THE
TRENT BRIDGE
BATTERY

The sporting Gunns: John, William (sitting), George and George Vernon (inset).

THE TRENT BRIDGE BATTERY

The Story of the Sporting Gunns

BASIL HAYNES
&
JOHN LUCAS

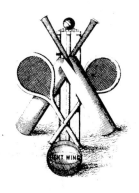

WILLOW BOOKS
Collins
8 Grafton Street, London W1
1985

ILLUSTRATION CREDITS

Thanks are due to the following individuals and organisations for allowing their photographs to be reproduced in this book:

Wilfred Baguley 20, 37, 54; BBC Hulton Picture Library 117, 180; David Frith Collection 36, 48, 53, 57; Gunn & Moore Ltd 131–137; Mrs Pauline Manders 95, 102, 179, 182, 185, 188, 190, 191, 195, 197; Roger Mann Collection 51, 82, 107–110; Nottinghamshire CCC 21, 32, 42, 121, 159, 163, 164, 166 (bottom); Nottingham Evening Post 127; Peter Townsend frontispiece, 63 (bottom), 67, 76, 77, 79, 80, 88, 97, 99, 102, 105, 118, 152, 154, 166 (top); Professor Derek West 38.

Willow Books
William Collins Sons & Co. Ltd
London · Glasgow · Sydney · Auckland
Toronto · Johannesburg

First published 1985
© Basil Haynes and John Lucas 1985

BRITISH LIBRARY CATALOGUING IN PUBLICATION DATA

Haynes, Basil
The Trent Bridge battery: the story of the
sporting Gunns.
1. Gunn (*Family*)   2. Sports – England
– Biography
I. Title   II. Lucas, John
796'.092'2   GV697.G/

ISBN 0-00-218175-4

Photoset in Linotron Sabon by
Rowland Phototypesetting Ltd
Bury St Edmunds, Suffolk
Made and printed in Great Britain by
William Collins Sons & Co. Ltd, Glasgow

CONTENTS

We wish to dedicate this book to
Judy, for her heartwarming tolerance of my addiction (B.H.)
and to
the abiding memory of Mr Fletcher's Particulars (J.L.)

FOREWORD

by Reg Simpson
Notts & England, Managing Director
of Gunn & Moore

I take much pleasure in writing the Foreword to *The Trent Bridge Battery* for two personal reasons.

First, I have a long and close association with Nottinghamshire County Cricket Club for which the exploits of the Gunn family – the taciturn double international William, the jovial allrounder John, the eccentric batting genius George, all test cricketers, and George junior – spanning some sixty years, form a great part of its cricketing history. William Gunn died the year after I was born, but I talked on many occasions to his nephews John and George and, as the authors reveal in this book, the Gunns' cricket is only half their fascinating story.

Second, a large part of my life, both as player and as bat maker, has been spent with Gunn & Moore, a firm which thrives as a memorial to the commercial acumen of William.

The firm has come a long way since 1885 when William Gunn and Thomas Moore put their training as employees in Richard Daft's sporting business to good use and opened their own sports emporium in modest premises at 6 Albert Street, Nottingham. Here, to cricket's great advantage, they went into the business of bat manufacture. The business flourished. By the time of William Gunn's death in 1921 the firm was internationally famous and today the factory and warehouse premises in Haslam Street, Nottingham, occupy more than an acre. William Gunn, from wherever he sits in a celestial pavilion, has much of which to be proud, although there is no longer any Gunn or Moore actively concerned with the firm which bears their names.

It is odd that in the very long list of cricket biographies the name of the Gunns has been absent until now. It is nicely appropriate though that such a strange omission should be rectified during Gunn & Moore's centenary year. Basil Haynes and John Lucas are deserving of considerable praise for producing such a delightfully interesting and eminently readable story of a family unique in the annals of cricket.

Acknowledgements

The writing of this work has been made possible by the help we received from a large number of people. We would like in particular to acknowledge the assistance of the following:

For interviews and reminiscences:
Mr R. D. F. Bland, Mrs A. E. Coulthard, Mr W. D. Gladdish, Mr Horace Murden, Mr Eric Penson, Mr H. Silverberg, Mr Frank Stokes, Mr Eric Terry, Mr Les Tomlinson, Mr A. J. Turner, Mr Albert Underwood, Mr Willis Walker.

For supplying other relevant material:
Mr Stephen Best, Mrs Pamela Blyth, Mr Grahame Booker, Mr Trevor Buck, Mr Mike Chappell, Mr David Frith, Mr Mike Frost, Mr Keith Gray, Mrs Judy Haynes, Mr F. E. Jenkins, Mr L. T. Lucas, Mr Robin McConnell, Mrs Florrie Pilkington, Mr Keith Pugh, Mr Jack Robertson, Professor Alistair Smart, Mr David Stapleton, Mr Paul Wain, Mr Keith Warsop, Mr Ken Wheatley, Canon D. H. Williams, Mr Peter Wright.

We wish especially to thank Jimmy Haynes and Joe Hardstaff for their splendidly full recollections; Peter Wynne-Thomas for sharing with us his encyclopaedic knowledge of Notts cricket; Roger Mann for allowing us access to his unrivalled archives of cricket; and Messrs Gunn & Moore for their generous assistance in this their centenary year.

We owe a great debt to members of the Gunn family: to Pauline Manders, G. V. Gunn's daughter; to Eric Gunn, John Gunn's son; and above all to Peter Townsend, John's grandson, without whose invaluable collection of family papers and unstinted co-operation this book could not have been written.

Basil Haynes and John Lucas
January 1985

INTRODUCTION

It is not difficult to think of families who have played cricket with distinction. The Graces, the Fosters, the Edriches, the Chappells, the Hadlees – these and many more come quickly to mind. Yet for a number of compelling reasons the Gunn family is the most remarkable of all. Four of them played cricket for Nottinghamshire. Three played for their country. One also played football at national level and was for years an important member of the Notts County side. One was perhaps the best-loved eccentric the game has ever known, a genius of inimitable gifts and personality whose memory is still dear to those who saw him play or who remember him in his private life, as devoted husband, absent-minded landlord, sardonic coach to local teams, and quirky but utterly endearing neighbour. All in all, there has never been a family quite like them.

The first to achieve fame was William and it is with him that the name Gunn becomes known beyond the boundaries of Nottinghamshire. He was born in 1858, in conditions of what must have been semi-poverty. Sixty-three years later, at the time of his death, he was famous as a great allround sportsman who had represented his country at both football and cricket; no less an authority than W. G. Grace had called him probably the finest professional batsman of his time; and he had founded and brought to prosperity the internationally known sports firm of Gunn & Moore. He left behind him two substantial houses and a considerable fortune; and his native city remembered him with awe if not affection as an astute man of business and a benefactor of Notts County Football Club whose president he had been and whose affairs he had put on a sound financial basis.

His two nephews, John and George, were made of rather different stuff. Unlike their uncle, who stood 6 feet 3 inches, both of the younger Gunns were on the short side, John stocky, George a mere bag of bones. Neither had the old man's business acumen. At various times in their lives they earned a penny or two from shop and pub-keeping, but they were never very well off. Nor does this seem to have bothered them. Indeed, it is probably true to say that John (born 1876) and George (born 1879) were supremely indifferent to money matters. What they cared about, from first to last, was cricket. As small boys they taught themselves how to play the game, when they were in their prime they were either playing or waiting to play, and in their old age they were at their most content when talking, arguing and reminiscing about the great days of the past, the matches in which they had played and the cricketers they had known. In his retirement George was never happier than when advising the small sons of his next-door neighbour on the need to play straight, without 'looking up to Jesus'. John's son recalls coming on his elderly father seated at the kitchen-table of his small house in West Bridgford – it was within hailing distance of Trent Bridge – a volume of *Wisden* propped up in front of him as he pored over averages, scores and results, either unaware of or indifferent to the fact that his dinner was burning in the oven. And on his deathbed . . . But that story must wait its proper moment.

Cricket, then, was their abiding concern. And yet it would not be true to say that the brothers had no other interests. As it happens, both were fine musicians. John possessed a pleasant baritone voice, while George regarded his tenor voice – although it was good enough – as of less importance than his skill as a pianist. It appears that in his youth he even contemplated a career on the concert platform and only reluctantly came to the conclusion that he would not do. (In the days of silent cinema and of regular concert parties it was by no means difficult to obtain regular work as an accompanist, but George aimed higher.) Both sang in the Lady Bay male voice choir and on his retirement from the first-class game George installed a Bechstein in the living quarters of the public house where he had become landlord, and which, by a curious coincidence, was the same public house from which his uncle had chosen a barmaid to be his second wife. There are many stories about George as landlord. But then there can be few cricketers about whom so many good stories have been told, retold, and carefully hoarded by those who knew this most unique of cricketers.

And it is as cricketers that the Gunns initially deserve attention. William was thought by many contemporaries to be an almost invulnerable batsman, so that it always came as a surprise when he got out. John developed into one of the finest allrounders of his era, while George, apart from being simply George – 'rare George Gunn' as Cardus called him – was undoubtedly one of the greatest opening batsmen of all time. His son, George Vernon, never achieved the fame of his elders. Nevertheless he was a regular member of that powerful Notts side from 1931 to the war, and he and George share the record of being the only father and son to score centuries in the same innings of a championship match. The records are, of course, significant. Between them in first-class cricket, the Gunns scored nearly 100,000 runs, made some 160 hundreds (including one by George, against Worcestershire, on his fiftieth birthday); and took 1,600 wickets. John is the only Notts cricketer to have scored 20,000 runs and taken 1,000 wickets; George scored 6,000 runs more than any other Notts batsman; and a Gunn still features in the highest second-, third-, fourth- and fifth-wicket partnerships for the county.

Yet, although they are important, records do not tell the half of it. How could they, when one is dealing with such variously gifted individuals? Besides, what happened to the Gunns off the field is frequently as interesting as the events on it. By interviewing and listening to the recollections of old friends, neighbours and, most important, family, we have been able to put together a composite biography which lays bare some of the ways by which professional sportsmen lived, how they brought up their children, cared for wives and families, and conducted themselves when they were not in flannels. In short, this book is not only about a great sporting family, it is also a piece of social history.

For over 60 years the family name of Gunn was associated with the first-class game. But after George's death in 1958 his brother brooded on the frailty of reputation. 'When I die, it'll all be forgotten,' he told his grandson, and it is understandable that, old and apparently ignored, he should have felt that time would obliterate all memory of the family's heyday. Yet more than any other game cricket thrives on memories of its past, and there is a very real sense in which the meaning of cricket can be arrived at only through its history. In that history the name of Gunn deserves an especially honoured place. The following book has been written in the hope that as long as the great game is played the Gunns will live.

1

BEGINNINGS

Normanton-on-the-Wolds is a small village which stands some ten miles to the south-east of Nottingham, just off the main road to Melton Mowbray. Although architecturally undistinguished – Pevsner does not mention it in his *Buildings of Nottinghamshire* and it lacks so much as a church – it is nevertheless a pretty enough place and in size at least can have changed little since 1820, when Anne, the wife of John Gunn, and living at 20 Main Street, gave birth to a baby boy. Anne was a local, as was her husband. In the census of 1848 John's profession is given as 'publican'. Ten years later he lists himself 'victualler'. Whether this indicates a downward shift in his fortunes is not certain, but it may well be so, and in view of the fact that several of the Gunn family were to be involved in the business of retailing drink it will do no harm to explain something of the laws governing its sale.

The Beer House Act of 1830 allowed more or less anyone to retail beer and cider. Its purpose was to prevent the unlicensed drinking of spirits which were thought to do harm. It did not include beer. If you wanted a licence you simply handed over two guineas to the licensing authorities, and that was that. But in 1834 the act was superseded by another, which for the first time introduced a distinction between 'on' and 'off' premises. To carry a licence for 'on' premise drinking – in other words, to class yourself as a publican – you now needed to produce to the Excise Officer a certificate of good character, signed by at least six ratepayers. The yearly cost of the licence was £3, and it must have been the possession of this licence which allowed John Gunn in 1841 to style himself 'publican'. 'Victualler' suggests that by 1851 he could either no longer afford the £3 licence, or that he had been denied a renewal of it. This was not unlikely, for during the troubled 1840s severe measures were taken against publicans who kept disorderly houses (which might often mean letting part of their premises for hire to radical groups) or who disobeyed the rule that made it illegal for public houses to be open between midnight on Saturday and noon on Sunday.

To return to the son. He had been given his father's name, and he grew up with a wheelwright's family for neighbours on one side and an agricultural labourer's on the other. Much of the work of the village was connected with agriculture, for Normanton-on-the-Wolds was, as it still is, in rural Nottinghamshire, and all about were farms, both great and small. If you were a lad in Normanton during the earlier part of the last century the chances were that you would either begin work as a farmboy and would graduate to general labourer or find employment through the use of more particular skills: hedging, ditching or thatching for instance. Moreover, the village and its immediate surrounds would mark the limits of your world. It is therefore in the way of such things that we should find John's younger brother, William, married to Sarah, the daughter of the neighbouring wheelwright, settled in the village as a blacksmith and living and working at 35 Main Street. (It is perhaps worth noting that, at the time William was establishing himself in his chosen trade, a small boy called Alfred Shaw was being paid half-a-crown a week to scare birds off a farmer's fields at Burton Joyce, a village five miles to the North of Nottingham.)

So much for work. What of games? John and William could have played cricket for their native village, for Normanton, like its near neighbour, Plumtree, had its own team at the time the boys were growing up. Unfortunately, we have no means of discovering whether John's interests ran in that direction. What we do know is that, unlike his brother, he chose to leave Normanton. Indeed, he had gone by 1841, and ten years later we find him living in the north Nottinghamshire mining village of Kimberley, at 155 Kimberley Flatt. By now he was married to Sarah, daughter of Thomas and Sarah Daley, he a stockman from Bleasby. The connections between Nottinghamshire cricket and mining are of course legendary, but as it happens the father of one of cricket's great legends was not working as a miner. Instead, he lists his occupation as 'porter in a brewery'.

In his *History of Nottingham* (1815), Blackman claims that 'it is partly owing to the excellent quality of the coal in the neighbourhood that Nottingham owes the superior flavour of its ale'. A strange claim perhaps, and yet the city and surrounding area is certainly well known for its splendid beers. W. T. Marchant's *In Praise of Ale* (1888) includes two spirited ballads which extol their virtues ('Nottingham ale, boys, Nottingham ale; No liquor on earth like Nottingham ale,' runs the refrain of one of them); and Kimberley has long been associated with brewing. Still, for John to have become a porter does not necessarily argue his devotion to beer. It does, however, suggest that he must have been a strong, well-built man, for no weakling could have toted around the vast barrels common to brewing in Victorian times. And given the fact that his brother William was a blacksmith we may infer that the Gunn genes found their way into John's son, for William Gunn, the cricketer, was, by common consent, not merely an exceptionally tall man, he was also an exceptionally strong one.

By 1851 the parents of William the cricketer already had two children: a daughter, Elizabeth, and a son called, inevitably it seems, John, who had been born in 1849, and who is of importance to this narrative because in course of time he would become father of John and George. Whatever became of porterage we do not know, but in 1858 the family moved to Nottingham, into the brand-new area of St Anne's where they set up residence in Cathcart Street, and where John was now described as 'licensed victualler and brewer'. It is unlikely that this move indicates any great upturn in his fortunes. It is, however, likely that, knowing something of the trade from his father's experiences, he decided on the move in order to take advantage of the rapid expansion of working-class estates, of which St Anne's was a typical example. Before 1845 the area was known as Clay Field. In that year it was enclosed and was made available for building land. The houses put up there were of the poorest type. According to one authority: 'Most . . . were of the same type and size, small houses intended for lower paid working classes. The street pattern is somewhat depressingly drawn in straight lines . . . and was no doubt designed to accommodate as many houses as possible, about 40 to the acre.'

A glance at the map of Nottingham shows that there were a number of factories in St Anne's, mostly concerned with the lace or dyeing industries, so there need be no mystery about the nature of work done by most of those who moved into the estate. The kind of house they lived in was described in a Board of Trade report for 1909:

> The five-roomed house is usually plain-fronted and built straight from the pavement line. It contains a parlour, about 12 feet by 11 feet by 9 feet, and a kitchen on the ground floor, two bedrooms on the first floor,

and above these a fifth room, which is sometimes an attic lit by a sky light . . . the street-door usually opens directly into the parlour. Behind the parlour is the kitchen and beyond that commonly a small scullery. There is as a rule a small back-yard and the back entrance . . . the water-closet and sometimes the coal-cellar are in the back yard.

It was in one such house that William Gunn was born.

The exact date of his birth is 4 December 1858. That much is certain. Sadly, however, we know tantalizingly little else about his earliest years, not even where he went to school. The family had left Cathcart Street by 1861, but the reason for their moving is a mystery. Had John Gunn's business failed? Did he hope for better things elsewhere? Did he perhaps see himself as a sutler to the growing army of workers brought into Nottingham by acts of enclosure and expanding industries, and spreading to areas other than St Anne's? We have no means of providing answers to these questions. All we can say is that the next firm evidence of the family's whereabouts comes first in 1862, when we know they were at 295 Russell Street, in Sherwood, and where they remained until at least 1864; and then in the 1881 census.

By this time John is dead, and his widow is therefore named as head of the house at 169 Kirk White Street, in the Meadows. Like St Anne's, the Meadows was land that had been developed for working-class housing during the latter half of the nineteenth century, and it is entirely possible that the Gunns moved there in the hope that it would help John to prosper in his trade. By the 1880s some fifteen thousand people lived and worked in the Meadows, so that it was a much larger community than St Anne's. (It reached to the River Trent at Trent Bridge in one direction, the Midland-London railway line in another.)

With the head of the family gone, the remaining members had to find a means of earning a living, and they did so in much the same ways as others of their class and circumstances were forced to do in the difficult years of the late nineteenth century: they set to and used whatever skills they had or could acquire. Sarah, John's widow, lists her occupation as 'laundress', Elizabeth is 'dressmaker', while two other daughters, Charlotte and Sarah Ann, describe themselves as 'teachers of music' — and, although it would be wrong to make too much of this in an age when all but the very poorest typically learned to play instruments and took for granted the fact that music formed the staple of home entertainment, it is nevertheless proper to note that the occupation of these two girls provides us with our first firm evidence about the musical accomplishment of the Gunns. And what of William? He gives his profession, simply enough, as 'cricketer'.

He was entitled to do so. In the previous year he had been taken onto Notts's books, and by 1881 he was an established member of the side. But to discover how this had come about we must return to his earlier days.

Whatever education William had and wherever he received it, it must at least have taught him to master the three Rs. We have seen letters from his later days which show that he wrote in a good, firm hand; and in view of his success as a businessman it is obvious that allied to native wit was a shrewd mastery of arithmetic, as well as of pounds, shillings and pence. We do not know whether any schoolmaster was responsible for encouraging his sporting abilities, but someone else certainly did. In a small pamphlet which Gunn & Moore put out in the early 1970s, describing the firm's history, William Gunn is credited with the cryptic remark that in his youth he had been much encouraged by the Rev. Joseph Stonehouse.

Stonehouse is a shadowy figure, but since he is important for our story it is as well to set down all we know about him. A Durham man by origin, he moved at the age of thirty-four from a curacy in Derby to become vicar of St Saviour's church in the Meadows. That was in 1872 and in all probability the Gunn family was by then already installed in Kirk White Street, for we shall see that during the following year William found employment in a manner which suggests that Stonehouse's influence was at work. The comparatively young vicar could have met the thirteen-year-old youth at local sports events, or at the church school in Glebe Street. Or perhaps William sang in the church choir? We know that in adult life he would entertain friends and fellow cricketers by dressing up and singing minstrel songs; and it is entirely possible that like so many boys of his age he learned the art of singing through early experiences in a church choir. It is also possible that by the time the Rev. Stonehouse first saw him he was playing cricket at good club level, and he would certainly have been watching it. For the Meadows was the home of one of the best club sides that the county of Nottingham has ever produced.

Castle Gate Cricket Club or, as it was later known, the Notts Castle Club, had its ground at Queen's Drive, a major road that cut through the heart of the Meadows and was no more than two minutes walk from Kirk

*Casual sport in the Meadows today. William no doubt learned the rudiments of
cricket and football on this grass.*

White Street. By the 1870s the club had become something of a nursery
for the county cricket club. It staged a number of top-class matches,
including games against MCC and Ground and important Midlands
clubs, and if at any time one of the matches was being played when Notts
were not themselves involved in a county game several of the county team
would be drafted in to strengthen the Castle Club. Some indication of its
fame can be gauged from the fact that, according to the *Nottingham
Journal* of 15 June 1878, when the club travelled to Liverpool to play a
two-day game against Birkenhead Park Club, 'there were about 10,000
persons waiting to see the match'; and we have discovered that during the
following year Skegness played host to a match between Lincolnshire
and Notts Castle, and that, again according to the *Nottingham Journal*,
'Mr R. Daft, who is one of the proprietors of the new ground, arranged
the match on the occasion of the opening.' In 1881, Arthur Shrewsbury

played on a fairly regular basis for Notts Castle, for reasons that will later become apparent. What more likely than that the young William Gunn and his older brother, John, should spend their free afternoons watching the club in action? We know that John was a keen cricketer, for in a fragment of autobiography his son John tells us that he used to watch his father play for Lenton United. And we may imagine that when they could not watch a game the two brothers would be busy practising, perhaps with that dogged devotion which William's nephews, John and George, were later to show as small boys, and which was to prove of such enormous benefit to them as they grew up.

We may also imagine John and William taking themselves whenever possible to Trent Bridge, a mere half mile from where they lived, and home to one of the greatest county sides, including as it did the likes of Richard Daft, John Jackson, Alfred and T. C. Shaw and William Oscroft.

> To what [asked Lillywhite's *Cricketers' Companion*] does the present champion county, Notts, owe its position? Is it not to the energetic way the Colts have been yearly trained, so that no sooner has a gap appeared in the ranks of the County Eleven than there have been half a dozen young players at hand fully qualified to fill the vacancy? Notts has always been famed for its supply of professionals and season after season closes with the County Eleven almost, if not quite, at the top of the tree.

It is very likely that William dreamed of emulating the famous men he saw in action, and whose exploits he would have heard and read about. (The *Nottingham Journal* carried long and extravagantly detailed accounts of the matches in which Notts were involved.) If so, he must have realized how great was the gap between the reality of Kirk White Street and the dream. Contemporary photographs show it for what it was: a long, straight, dingy street of poor-quality terraced houses, low-lying and liable to flooding. (In the great flood of 1875 a journalist reported that 'In parts of Queen's Road, Arkwright Street and Kirkwhite Street, people were conveyed to and fro in carts'.) Life in such circumstances must have been very much a struggle for survival. And what was he going to do about finding work? There was of course the Midland Railway Company, which gave work to many men from the estate. There was Clifton Colliery, a mere stone's throw away at Wilford Bridge, which had opened in 1870 and which employed over a thousand men and boys from the Meadows and Wilford Village. There was Turney

*Scenes during the great flood of 1875. Above, the view from the Railway Bridge,
Carrington Street; below, a train entering the Midland Station. Kirk White Street lay
between the railway and the River Trent.*

◆ ● ◆

Brother's Factory at Trent Bridge itself, a large and successful engineer-
ing works which had been established in 1862. And nearer the town
centre there were the lace factories. Choice of a kind, maybe, and a choice
that his friends were forced to make, but certainly not one to quicken the
pulse.

As matters turned out, however, the boy was not required to choose.

> At the age of 14 [William Gunn] entered the service of Mr Richard Daft,
> as an assistant in the Cricket Outfitting business, and no doubt his
> coming into contact with many notable cricketers gave an additional
> impetus to his natural yearnings for a cricketer's life. He displayed
> remarkable ability in determining the weight of a bat, and was fond of
> practising a favourite cut or drive, sometimes in the shop, and much to
> the detriment of the windows.

This account is given by C. H. Richards in his pamphlet on Gunn and,
sparse as it is, it is the only one we have of William's entry into the world

of work. (In his *Nottinghamshire Cricket and Cricketers* F. S. Ashley-Cooper more or less repeats it verbatim and clearly has no other source of information for his portrait.) But someone must have recommended the youth to Daft, and that someone would surely have been the Rev. Stonehouse?

It seems reasonable to suppose that Stonehouse saw in William the possibility of future greatness and wanted to do his best to ensure that the youth should not be lost to the game. Richards, it is true, says that William's opportunities for practice were few and that 'it was only by sheer determination that he succeeded in improving his acquaintance with cricket', but this seems less than just to his employer. After all, Daft was not only one of the greatest batsmen of his time, he had become captain of the county in 1871 in succession to Parr and, having taken Gunn into his outfitting business, it is most unlikely that he would have left him to moulder there, knowing as he must have done about the boy's

◆ ● ◆

Richard Daft, whose outfitting business William joined at the age of 14.

talents. Besides, the suggestion that he was a hard taskmaster, or indifferent to William's promise – perhaps even jealous of it – goes clean counter to everything else that we know about him. In Ashley-Cooper's words, 'from first to last he enjoyed the respect of all with whom he had dealings . . . It has been well said that everybody trusted him, respected him, honoured the man and admired the cricketer.' Daft's benefit match – North v. South at Trent Bridge in 1876 – was recalled by one of the umpires, Thoms, as a unique occasion. 'I have,' he said, 'during the past twenty years been planted in some big rings, but never before saw a more densely-packed and enthusiastic body of spectators . . . Cricketers of all denominations were there, from the "rising star" to the matured and past.' Daft's benefit game was, he adds, 'an event which will always be mentioned as a red-letter day in the annals of cricket.' And the following year the *Nottingham Journal* wrote about this much-loved man that,

> no better example for a young professional can be furnished than is to be found in the high reputation of Richard Daft . . . Independent, loyal to his country (*sic*), always willing to aid when aid has been wanted and never overlooking in the quest of its pursuit as a profession the fact that cricket is meant to be a game, Daft stands out as the best model of what a professional cricketer can be . . .

Daft had started his business some years previously, and it eventually became not merely an outfitters but a kind of agency, supplying cricketers of particular skills to whoever wanted them, even to the extent of dispatching spin bowlers to India in response to telegrams from importunate Nabobs. From all we know and have read about him it seems clear that he was an ideal employer and that the work which Gunn was called on to do formed ideal employment for an aspiring cricketer. It is characteristic of the man that in his inimitable *Kings of Cricket* (1893) Daft should praise Gunn, while claiming no part in his development. 'I have always been a great admirer of his play,' he says, and 'have always watched with interest his career.'

It was a career that took some time to develop. As we have seen, Richards implies that this was because Daft kept him always in the shop. In all probability Richards is thereby trying to find an explanation for the fact that Gunn was a slow starter. Ashley-Cooper goes one better. According to him, 'regular match-practice was denied' Gunn and so, 'as a result of a conversation between his father and Mr Henry Turner, the Honorary Secretary to the Notts Castle CC, it was decided to allow

[William] to adopt the game as a profession.' There are several reasons why this account, for which Ashley-Cooper provides no firm evidence, will hardly do. In the first place we do not know when Gunn began playing for Notts Castle, but it can hardly have been as a professional, unless he had made a name for himself at another club, which Ashley-Cooper has himself declared to be an impossibility. This is not to say that local clubs did not employ professionals. They had been doing so for some considerable time. In 1862, for example, Alfred Shaw was paid to play for Grantham. But it is inconceivable that Notts Castle would have paid Gunn to play for them until and unless they knew he was an exceptionally good cricketer. That can hardly have been before the late 1870s, and the idea that the club secretary and William's father would then solemnly sit down to discuss the future of a man of twenty is extremely unlikely. It is also, of course, made even more ridiculous by the fact that at the time William is known to have been playing for Notts Castle his father was already dead.

We have discovered that in 1879 William played for a club called simply Meadow. On Monday 7 July, he opened the batting for them against Midland Star and scored 18. On 18 August he went in at number eight against East Leake and Ruddington, and managed only 2; and the following Monday, in the return match against Midland Star, he was stumped when he had scored 4. His brother John also played in this match, batting at number six and being out without scoring. The scores in these matches are all low, suggesting that the quality of cricket and/or of the pitches was poor; and Gunn does nothing in them to encourage one to feel that a young genius is about to burst from cover. Quite the contrary, in fact. A mere glance at the few occasions when he appears in print during these years will enforce the notion that he was a very average club cricketer. Given Daft's credentials and the fact that he obviously had some influence over Notts Castle (hence the visit to Skegness in 1879, already referred to), it is virtually certain that it was he who persuaded the club to take Gunn on. He must have seen in the young cricketer qualities which are not revealed in the mere scores we have been able to find for him. Not very much is known of what went on in the years leading up to William's being taken onto the Notts books, but it seems obvious that Daft did all he could to help the young man.

Whatever the facts of Gunn's apprentice years, there can be no doubt that 1880 was crucial. On 8 May of that year he scored 107 for Notts Castle

23

against Melton Mowbray. Two days later he appeared at Lord's for Colts of England v MCC where he made an undefeated 32, the highest score on either side, and one that so pleased the MCC authorities that he was immediately offered, and accepted, the position of ground bowler at Lord's. On 17 May he was drafted into the Notts Colts side as a last-minute replacement and made 70 against Yorkshire Colts, the first of his important innings at Trent Bridge. Shortly afterwards he scored 90 for Notts Castle against Wollaton, and as a result was offered a trial in the county team. On 3 June he played his first match for Notts, against Surrey at Trent Bridge, and scored 13 not out and 9. He was on his way.

Or was he? For as so often happens, a bright beginning was followed by discouragement and failure. Although he played in all the county's matches that season, he finished with the decidedly poor average of 10.13 from 16 completed innings. The lowest point was reached in the match against Yorkshire, at Sheffield, where he was twice out without scoring. According to Richards, the high point 'was in the memorable match at the Oval, when Surrey were dismissed for 16 runs, his score, of 29 not out, upon that occasion being an excellent display.'

If Alfred Shaw is to be believed, Gunn needed to do well in that match. In his *Reminiscences*, he recalls that,

> There was a circumstance in William Gunn's early days that I recall with special pleasure, for it may be said to have started him on his great career. At the commencement of his connection with Notts county he was not a success. He had failed so often that the Notts Committee, I learned, had decided that if he did not succeed in a certain match he must be dropped. He again failed to do much in the first innings, but in the second I sent him in early and told him to 'play up'. He scored 29 and the runs were so well got that his title to a place in the Notts team was never again questioned. The match was against Surrey, in the year 1880.

Although the story has probably lost nothing in the telling, it is obviously true that in his first season of county cricket Gunn was not a conspicuous success. Yet it is also apparent that despite various setbacks his reputation was advancing and that certain authorities persisted in regarding him as a cricketer with a great future. Why else should he have been chosen to play for the Under Thirty side against the Over Thirty at Lord's – he scored 15 and 6 not out; and why else should Notts have continued to include him in their team, in spite of his poor form? The answer to these questions may well lie with Daft, in his last season as Notts' captain, but still their most revered and respectfully listened-to player. It seems very likely that it was Daft who told the committee to persevere with the young man who in many ways he might well regard as his protégé, and equally likely that it was Daft who brought Gunn's name to the attention of others.

From all we can discover those others seem to have shared Daft's view of the matter. Not only did Gunn play in representative matches at a time when his achievements can hardly have recommended themselves to the notice of many. There is also the fact that Ashley-Cooper, who, whatever his failings, clearly knew a good deal about the goings-on of those years, writes that 'At first [Gunn's] play was neither as graceful nor as sound as it was a few seasons later, but the critics agreed that he was destined to take a high place in the game provided he persevered.'

Persevere he certainly did, and to such good effect that for Notts in the following season he finished with an average of 24.15 from twenty completed innings. These included 74 against Sussex at Trent Bridge, in the opening match of the season, and 68 against Surrey, also at Trent Bridge, an innings which was described in the *Nottingham Journal* 'as one of the best innings ever seen at the Bridges. His hitting was singularly fine – clean, hard, and well placed, and his defence masterly.' He also played what Richards called a 'magnificent' innings of 91 in the return match against Sussex, at Brighton. For MCC that season he scored two centuries: 109 against Mote Park at Maidstone and 105 against Notts and District at Burton-on-Trent. To complete a memorable year he played his first match for the Players against the Gentlemen at the Oval, and although he failed with the bat he distinguished himself by his agile fielding and in particular by a wonderful overhead catch to dismiss A. N. Hornby. 'Bad luck, Monkey,' a member said as the unlucky batsman stumped his way up the pavilion steps. 'Ay,' Hornby grunted, 'no one but a damned giraffe would have got near it.'

Yet Notts cricket in 1881 was far less remarkable for events on the field than for those that took place off it, and since historians of the game have until now been more or less silent about the extraordinary happenings of that season it will be as well to pause a little over them. Richards, it is true, refers to 'the defection of several of the leading professionals', and Ashley-Cooper demurely mentions 'an unfortunate schism'; but Daft does not discuss the matter, nor does E. V. Lucas in his *A Hundred Years of Trent Bridge*, and it is also ignored by Altham and Swanton in what is in many ways the definitive history of cricket. Odder still, Shaw says nothing about it in his *Reminiscences*. In his three-page chapter on his career with Notts he tells us that he played his first game for the county, against Kent, on 13 and 14 June 1864, and his last, against Yorkshire, in June 1887. What he does not reveal is that his career with the county might have come to an end some six years earlier. For in 1881 Shaw and six other players were to all intents and purposes sacked by the county committee.

How did this crisis come about? The only detailed account of the matter we have been able to discover is not surprisingly in the pages of the *Nottingham Journal*. On Saturday 4 June, the newspaper ran a leading article under the heading 'Trades Unionism in the Cricket World'. It began as follows:

> It is with considerable regret – regret which we are sure will be shared by all who are interested in the manly game – that we have to announce that the differences between the committee of the County Cricket Club, and seven of the players have reached a crisis, and that when Notts took the field at Manchester on Thursday, against the county of Lancashire, a number of well-known names were missing from the Eleven.

Two days later, on Monday 6 June, the *Journal* published what purported to be the entire correspondence between the executive of the county committee and Shaw and Shrewsbury, and on the following Monday a long letter from Shaw appeared in the newspaper, explaining as fully as possible his and the other players' views of how the crisis had come about. What follows is a summary of how trades unionism reached the cricket world.

The affair begins with a letter from the county secretary, Henry Holden, to Arthur Shrewsbury, in which Holden says he has been informed that,

> you have arranged, or are about to arrange, a match Nottinghamshire v Yorkshire, to be played at Bradford. I therefore think it best to write at once, and say that the committee strongly and decidedly object to any county match being arranged by anybody, except those home and home (*sic*) matches arranged at the annual meeting of county secretaries at Lord's.

In a terse, carefully worded but barbed reply, Shaw and Shrewsbury claim that theirs is not a bona fide county match, since they will be selecting the Notts side.

The next important development comes in a letter dated 16 March, which Holden seems to have sent to seven players, Shaw, Shrewsbury, Selby, Morley, Barnes, Flowers and Scotton. He is instructed to ask them whether they will be willing to play in the Colts match, 'giving your services gratuitously as usual', and furthermore whether 'you will agree to play in any match for the county for which you may be selected, on the usual terms, viz. £5 for matches lost or drawn, £6 for matches won.' In addition to this, the players are to undertake 'not to accept any engagement to play in any County match styled Nottingham v any other County, such match not having been arranged by the County Committee.' To this Shaw and Shrewsbury reply that before they and the other players are prepared to give their agreement to these conditions they wish to know why they have been engaged for only one match rather than for the whole season, whether the committee will be prepared to guarantee a benefit to any player who has completed ten years with the club or whether, failing that, the committee will at least 'express an opinion that the players are entitled to one', and whether the committee will agree to the arranged match against Yorkshire being played, providing that the Notts team is styled 'an Eleven of Nottingham selected by A. Shaw'.

Attitudes now hardened. The committee would agree to none of the players' proposals, although it did attempt to divide and conquer by offering to engage all but Flowers and Scotton for the season, and Holden extended an olive branch of sorts by suggesting that Shaw might like to call his team 'Alfred Shaw's Eleven'. To their credit, Shaw and Shrewsbury stood by the lesser players. Either all were to be offered terms or none would play. The result was that none played. More letters were exchanged, but the upshot was that throughout the 1881 season Notts had to manage without two of their greatest players.

What lies behind the dispute is a player's right to protect his means of livelihood. This was not of course how the *Nottingham Journal* saw the matter. The newspaper's leader of 4 June hints darkly that,

there are influences at work which have induced the players to look out for fresh grievances . . . The dispute has cost a great deal of trouble and anxiety to the committee, who are mostly men of position and well up in cricket, and who would not dream of doing a professional any injury. 27

Perhaps not, but the fact is that the committee was not prepared to guarantee benefit matches to cricketers who surely had a perfect right to expect that they would receive one, and that they demanded total loyalty from players while refusing to guarantee those same players a season's contract. Suppose you fell ill, or lost form, or suppose that matches were rained off? What then? Nothing. Those men of position were not required to compensate players for their lost incomes.

In such circumstances it is hardly to be wondered at that two such senior players as Shaw and Shrewsbury should stand out for better terms. Besides, the previous year they had established their own Sports Outfitters business, in Carrington Street, Nottingham, and they no doubt felt that with this financial cushion beneath them they could afford to take on the committee without risking a hard bump.

So much may be granted them. But is it possible to defend their decision to sell their names and that of the county by arranging the match against Yorkshire? Was not it a needlessly provocative gesture, even though it was bound to guarantee a decent income for all who took part? Not really. For as Shaw was quick to point out, the committee had made no similar protest when in 1873 Richard Daft had arranged just such a match. True, the committee had eventually entered an objection, but only at the close of the season when it appeared that the match, which Notts had lost, might be treated as a first-class fixture and thus cost them the championship title. And anyway all round the country players were giving their names to matches to make a little extra money for themselves and their colleagues.

In the long run the affair, acrimonious as it was, helped both the players and the club. All seven were reinstated for the following season, and Notts once again became an all-powerful side. In the short run, the troubles of 1881 undoubtedly helped William Gunn establish himself in the county eleven. By now he seems to have become exclusively a sportsman. 'Cricketer' he lists himself in the 1881 census, and cricketer he most certainly was. But he was also a footballer. In Volume 14 of their *Victorian Nottingham: A Story in Pictures*, Richard Iliffe and Wilfred Baguley deal with the rise of football in the city; and among other things they remark that in 1881 Notts County suffered from a financial crisis. (Could it have been that players were demanding more money – there were no formal contracts, but the winds of change at Trent Bridge might have blown across to the Meadows?) Matters quickly improved, however, and 'the famous William Gunn, who had been playing with

Nottingham Forest, decided to join Notts County, who also at this time left their ground in the Meadows to play their home matches on a portion of the fine Trent Bridge cricket ground.'

There is a puzzle here, because nobody seems to know very much about Gunn's career with the Forest. (Football club records, it has to be said, are notoriously sketchy.) What is certain is that both Forest and Notts County were very much local sides. In 1880 Forest's home ground was at Trent Bridge (the previous season they had been in the Meadows), while Notts County played at the Castle Cricket Ground. It would therefore have been easy for William to have joined either club, and he could have been playing for some years prior to 1880, because in that era most of the games took place on Thursday afternoons, which was early closing day in Nottingham and therefore a half-day for Mr Daft's assistant. Richards, who is clearly not much interested in such matters, reports that 'Gunn was one of the finest Association football players in the kingdom. His favourite position,' he adds, 'was outside left forward.'

He was shortly to become an international footballer. He was also about to prove himself one of the greatest of English batsmen.

2
PROMISE AND ACHIEVEMENT

If we know little about William Gunn's career with Nottingham Forest the explanation is simple: he was not a regular member of their first eleven. According to the historian of Nottingham football, Keith Warsop, he joined the club after Notts Castle FC disbanded in 1878. However, apart from playing in the FA Cup match against Aston Villa in November 1881, he did not begin to make a name for himself as a footballer until he joined Notts County. His first game for his new club was against Stoke, at the Castle ground, where he appeared at right back. He played one other game for County's first team during the season of 1881–82. Then it was back to cricket.

There is little need to linger over the 1882 season. The seven rebels returned and Nottinghamshire were once again a mighty team. At the end of the season they were placed equal first with Lancashire. William Gunn's own career did not, however, advance far. His best score was a modest enough 39 against Yorkshire, at Sheffield, and he finished with an average of 11.73 for fifteen completed innings. As part compensation for these disappointing figures, we may note that he occasionally proved useful as a change bowler (in the match against Gloucestershire, at Clifton, he took five wickets for 38 runs); and he scored two centuries for MCC: 103 against Buxton and 188 against Somerset. Yet it was clearly a poor season for a cricketer from whom so much was expected. What is interesting is that few seriously doubted his potential, and this is revealed in a touching anecdote recorded by Ashley-Cooper. When the visiting Australians came to play Notts at Trent Bridge, 'Oscroft, in the most sporting manner, asked the committee to allow Gunn to take his place in the team, saying he was the better man. They did so and allowed Oscroft his fee.' Which speaks well both for the committee and, particularly, for Oscroft. Unfortunately, there is no fairy tale ending to the story. The match was spoiled by the weather, and Gunn had no chance to distinguish himself.

He did distinguish himself in the football season that followed. In 1882–83 he became an established member of the Notts County side. The tall, powerfully built man played regularly at outside right and occasionally on the opposite wing. In all, he turned out for twenty-two games, scored fourteen goals, and was in the side that met and was beaten 2-1 by Old Etonians at Kennington Oval in the Cup semi-finals. Gunn was, of course, still officially working for Richard Daft, but by now he was more use to his employer as advertising material and contact man than for the hours he put in behind the counter or at his ledger. Still, he needed the work. He could not be officially paid for his football. Professionalism in that sport did not begin until 1885. On the other hand there is no doubt that in common with most other regular players he would have been paid bootmoney; and given the fact that his tremendous turns of speed and the power of his shooting were bringing large crowds to the County games it was in the club's interest to look after him as well as they could.

In April 1883, William Gunn reported back to Trent Bridge. It was to be a crucial season for him. The tag of 'promising' was beginning to wear a little thin. Could he justify the faith so many had in him, or would he come to be one of those many talented cricketers who, for a variety of reasons, never achieve the fame and glory that have been predicted for them? Gunn was lucky to be playing for so powerful a county as Notts. There was such strength in the batting and bowling that the committee could afford to nurse along one or two players whom less richly endowed counties would have had to sacrifice. Yet he must have known that he could not expect to survive another full season unless he scored runs and scored them consistently. And that is exactly what he did. In eighteen completed innings he scored 455 runs at an average of 25.28. He also took ten wickets for 199 runs. Not dazzling, perhaps, but good enough to put him fifth in the Notts batting averages, behind Barnes, Shrewsbury, Flowers and Selby; and also good enough to still the worst fears that he might be no more than a nine-days wonder. His best scores were 52 against Middlesex, 46 and 77 in the match against Gloucestershire (his 77 included thirteen boundaries), 52 and 68 in the match against Sussex at Brighton (eleven boundaries in the 68) and 42 against Yorkshire at Sheffield, the top score in a match played on an increasingly difficult wicket.

At the end of the season the county were placed in first position. Yorkshire complained, on the grounds that they had lost two matches

Notts, County Champions 1883. Left to right, standing: W. Barnes, F. Brown (sec), A. Shrewsbury, E. Mills, W. H. Scotton, J. Selby; sitting, W. Wright, W. Attewell, A. Shaw, W. Gunn; front, M. Sherwin, W. Flowers.

out of sixteen played, whereas Notts had lost one out of twelve played; but the rules of the day made it quite clearly Notts's season. Lillywhite's *Cricketers' Companion* remarked that the county's success was entirely owing to men 'bred and born in the county itself', and that Lancashire, one of the counties challenging Notts for supremacy, owed a good deal to Notts-born players. For where, Lillywhite asked in his somewhat awkward style, 'would this county have been without Wm McIntyre in the past and Crossland and Briggs at the present? . . . [Apart from Notts] it is in the power of no other county but Yorkshire to raise eleven professional players who year after year play for their county – real Nottingham men, born there, living there, and working there.'

Lying behind these apparently innocent sentences is the ghost of an acrimonious affair that merits a brief mention. Nottinghamshire's only defeat in 1883 had been at the hands of Lancashire, and Lancashire's victory was almost wholly due to the bowling of Crossland. What made this particularly galling was the fact that Crossland was not strictly qualified to play for Lancashire against his own home county and also that he was thought not to deliver the ball fairly. Feelings between the two counties ran so high, charge and counter-charge were so intense, that for several seasons they refused to play each other. Lancashire sent Notts a Christmas Card for 1883–84 which drew up 'Rules for Matches between the two counties':

Rule 1 That in playing Lancashire the Lancashire men shall not be allowed to use bats but only broom handles
Rule 2 That Lancashire shall not be allowed any bowlers, and if so no stumps to be used; and the Notts captain to select the bowler
Rule 3 That both umpires shall be strictly Notts men
Rule 4 That in case there is any fear that Notts should lose, even under these rules, the Notts men do leave the field and refuse to finish the game

On New Year's Day 1884, Lancashire received a New Year's Greetings Card, which read as follows: 'The only rules for players of the County Eleven are that they shall neither have been born in nor reside in Lancashire. Sutton-in-Ashfield men will have the preference.'

By the time that card was sent William Gunn was deeply into the football season. He played in thirty-one games for Notts County during the winter of 1883–84, scored a modest ten goals, and made another appearance in the FA Cup semi-final, against Blackburn Rovers at Aston Villa's ground, and was again on the losing side, Blackburn winning 1-0. That game was played on 1 March 1884. A fortnight later, and having earlier taken part in the trial match, North v South, at Kennington Oval, Gunn was selected to play inside right for England against Scotland at Glasgow, where the home team won by the only goal of the match. Two days later, and now at inside left, he took the field for England against Wales at Wrexham. This time England won 4-0, and Gunn scored one of the goals.

As a result of his feats on the sportsfield Gunn was now something of a local celebrity. He was also a married man. In October 1883, he had married Anne Elizabeth Sewell, a local girl, and the couple set up home at 54 Lamcote Grove. Footballer and cricketer, newly and happily married,   33

54 Lamcote Grove.

with a safe career in the shop of a respected cricketer and now wealthy businessman: it must have seemed to William Gunn, at the opening of the 1884 cricket season, that he had come a long way from those early days in St Anne's and the Meadows. He could hardly have guessed what lay ahead. And had he been of a gloomy turn of mind he might a little later have thought that the best was already behind him. For the season began in disastrous manner. In the opening match of the season, against Sussex, at Trent Bridge, he was out for nought in his single innings. In the following match, against Middlesex at Lord's, he went one worse, this time collecting a pair. Matters improved a little when he made 44 against Surrey. Yet at the end of ten completed innings, including 19 and 8 against the Australians, his average was a paltry 8.00.

The return match against Sussex was played at Brighton. The weather was good, there was a large crowd, and Gunn and Shrewsbury provided the entertainment. They put on 266 runs for the fifth wicket and when Gunn was out he had scored 122, including seventeen boundaries. Shrewsbury went on to make 209, but that splendid score was of less significance for English cricket than Gunn's century. He had at last played the innings of which his faithful supporters had believed him capable, and in doing so he had shown such mastery that during its course every Sussex player bar the wicketkeeper had been given the chance to try to dismiss him.

He had done it once. Now, could he do it again? The return match against Middlesex was played at Trent Bridge. In front of his own crowd Gunn scored 138, the highest as well as the best innings he had played for his county. He was at the wicket for four hours 55 minutes, he hit sixteen boundaries and he did not give a chance. The following week the Australians returned to Trent Bridge. Gunn scored a superb 68, driving with power and precision. By the time the season ended, he had scored 537 runs in county matches for an average of 28.26. Considering the way he had started, it was a very fine achievement, and it led Shaw and Shrewsbury to invite him to join their party for the forthcoming Australian tour.

No doubt to their amazement, Gunn turned the offer down. Several factors were at work. In the first place he was, after all, a newly married man. Secondly, he must surely have hoped to play a great deal more international football. Yet if he went with Shaw and Shrewsbury he would be away for the whole of the football season. Thirdly, and perhaps most importantly, he was busy setting up his own business.

Towards the end of the nineteenth century interest in sport was rapidly expanding. Many people watched, many more played. From junior schools up to universities, from local church clubs up to the mighty city and county teams, cricket, football, rugger, and the as yet lesser sports such as rowing, tennis, golf, shooting and archery: all were on the increase. England had become a sports-mad nation. As a result businesses that manufactured and sold sporting equipment began to spring up in every town. Nottingham already had two such distinguished businesses: Richard Daft's and Shaw and Shrewsbury's. It was now to have its third, and the one which, in name at least, has proved the most permanent of all.

Early in 1885 the firm of Gunn & Moore opened its first modest premises, at 6 Albert Road (it was soon to move to the site on Carrington Street where it would stand for many years). Thomas James Moore was a cashier who, like his new partner, had previously worked for Richard Daft, as had their first employee, Joseph Stirland. It is unlikely that Daft would have objected to the new firm. As we have already noted he was by now a wealthy man and there was room in the city for a third sports business; besides, he would have appreciated Gunn's desire to give himself the financial security that neither cricket nor football could guarantee. And if we may judge from the unalloyed warmth with which he writes about Gunn in *Kings of Cricket* (1893) the new business venture did not adversely affect relationships between the two men.

Almost from the first the business prospered. No doubt Gunn's reputation as allround sportsman helped, and at least some of the contacts he and Moore had made while they were in Daft's employ proved useful to them in their new position; and, to anticipate a little, there was another reason why the firm so quickly began to succeed. Almost directly opposite their premises in Carrington Street was a public house, kept by Mordecai Sherwin, the seventeen-stone Notts wicket-keeper. Mordecai had a son, William, who loved cricket but had no

Mordecai Sherwin.

The Victoria Hotel, which subsequently changed its name to the Bentinck. In the background can be seen the sports firm of Shaw & Shrewsbury. The original 1885 site of Gunn & Moore was just across from the Victoria.

◆ ● ◆

aptitude for the game. The youth had therefore been apprenticed to a batmaker and having learnt his trade returned to Nottingham where his father set him up in a workshop in the pub's back yard to manufacture cricket bats. At first Gunn & Moore had bought their bats from London. Now they made an offer for William Sherwin's small factory, installed him as foreman, and gave him a free hand to develop his considerable skills as a batmaker. Thus the great tradition of Gunn & Moore bats was established.

A Select XI – including William Gunn – which, as far as is known, never took the field. This beautiful picture was the subject of an article by Professor Derek West in The Cricketer, *January 1985.*

William's career as businessman opened at the time that his career as England footballer closed. In that season of 1883–84 he played in thirty games for Notts County and scored sixteen goals. But he was not asked to play in any international trial match, and, although he was to be chosen for North v South in January 1886, those two games of March 1884 were the only occasions on which he played international football. Did he mind? We have no means of knowing. He was by nature taciturn, slightly withdrawn, as exceptionally tall men often are. He had acquaintances and even some friends, but he seems always to have guarded against making frank disclosures of his feelings. And if he did feel some disappointment it must have been partly made up for by the next time he came to wear a Notts County football shirt.

The summer of 1885 was when William Gunn the cricketer finally came into his own. It was a season during which the weather played havoc with a number of fixtures, and throughout the summer wickets were unpredictable. What is important about Gunn's performances, therefore, is less his actual scores than the consistency with which he succeeded and the fact that he was so often his team's best batsman, managing not merely to stay in but to take control of bowling that had proved far too good for his team-mates.

He was now in his twenty-eighth year, physically at his peak, emotionally matured by marriage and a business career, and with the experience of several seasons of county cricket behind him. The dourness of his early days had been replaced by a sound defence and a readiness to attack bowling that was slightly less than perfect in line and length. His great reach and power meant that, if he decided, he could get away with strokes that would cost less well endowed batsmen their wicket. And in the wet, uncertain summer of 1885, he did so decide.

Apropos of this it is worth noting that, in his *Golden Age of Cricket*, Robert Trumble remarks that he is certain his father, Hugh Trumble, modelled his batting style on William Gunn.

> The latter possessed a rather unique stroke for a ball pitched well up on the off. It was neither a cover drive nor a slash past point, but something between the two, and not a suitable shot apparently for a batsman other than one possessing a long reach and a powerful physique.
>
> My father often demonstrated the stroke to me and I recall it very well. Stepping well out of the crease with a quick and very forward placement of the left leg down the wicket and towards the flight of the ball, the bat was brought back steeply and the half-drive, half-slash

stroke aimed with great force at the ball. I can imagine that if contact were made as intended very few fieldsmen within range would have much chance of stopping the ball.

Armed with this stroke and others, William Gunn set about the country's bowlers. In the first match of 1885, against Sussex at Trent Bridge, he scored 44 and then 63, the latter a particularly brilliant, aggressive innings. In the following match, against Surrey, he was Notts's top scorer with 57. Against Yorkshire at Bramall Lane he made 33 and then 88. 'An innings of exceptional merit' was how this second innings was described, as was his 59 not out at the Oval 'made in a very bad light'. By the end of the season he had scored 627 runs from 19 completed county innings, and at an average of 33.00.

But what made the nation at large take note of Gunn's extraordinary talent were his performances for MCC. Against Oxford University he scored 71, followed that with 44 against Sussex, made 111 against Suffolk and 103 not out against Wiltshire and, in a different vein, had match figures of eleven for 85 when he bowled for the club against Hampshire. (It is tempting to speculate on just how good an allrounder Gunn would have made had he been prepared, or able, to persist with his bowling.) Above all, there was the game against Yorkshire, played at Lord's. In their first innings MCC managed 148 and then dismissed Yorkshire for a poor 69. When they batted a second time the MCC score had reached 72 for 3 when Gunn and Barnes came together. Four hours 40 minutes later the score was 402 for 4 and Gunn was on his way back to the pavilion, bowled for 203. Barnes went on to score 140 not out, but there was never any doubt in the minds of either the spectators or the Yorkshire team as to whose innings had been the outstanding one. True, Gunn gave two difficult chances, but the combined power and elegance of his hitting (twenty fours and two sixes) and the unvaried mastery with which he played all the bowlers Yorkshire tried against him were proof of greatness.

It is small wonder that Gunn now began to play regularly in important representative games. He took part in two of the three matches against Shaw's Australian team and also played twice for North v South. He was in all three of the Gentlemen–Players matches, scoring 93 at the Oval (easily the top score by any player in the three games) and 82 at Scarborough. Overall, during the summer of 1885 Gunn scored 1,451 runs from 40 completed innings, finishing with an average of 36.28.

From July 1885 it became legal for football clubs to employ professionals. As soon as his cricket duties allowed, William Gunn was registered as professional with Notts County. During the season that followed he played in twenty-three games for the club and scored eleven goals. He also produced a career-best performance during that season when, in the second round of the FA Cup, he scored three times against the Sheffield Club. And yet it is difficult to avoid the feeling that football was becoming of far less importance in his life than cricket. True, one more full season lay ahead, that of 1887–88, when he played in twenty-nine games and scored eleven goals. But that season apart he began to feature less frequently in the Notts County team. He was to play his last game for the club in 1893, against Aston Villa, by which time he would have played in 144 matches and scored sixty-four goals. His great days as a footballer were over from the mid-1880s.

As far as cricket was concerned it was a very different story. That summer of 1885 altered everything, for it not only spectacularly confirmed other people's good opinion of him, it allowed him to believe in himself. In the years that followed his prowess came to be such that he can fairly be called one of the great cricketers of his or any other age. Among his best innings of 1886 were 83 in the second innings against Middlesex at Lord's, top score and crucial to Notts's five-wicket victory; 82 against Gloucestershire at Moreton-in-the-Marsh (he kept Shrewsbury company for much of the time that the great man was scoring 227) and 80 not out in the return match at Trent Bridge; and top score of 70 in Notts's final game against Kent. He also scored a fine 43 for Players of England against the touring Australians at Bradford.

Whether that innings had much to do with the matter is unknown, but in any event Shaw and Shrewsbury renewed their invitation to Gunn to tour Australia with their team, and this time he accepted. This virtually guaranteed his entry into international cricket since the touring party consisted of only twelve players. Seven came from Notts, a fact which reflects not only the tour organizers' county, but the pre-eminence of its cricketers. In addition to Shaw, Shrewsbury and Gunn, Sherwin, Barnes, Scotton and Flowers all went. They were joined by Barlow and Briggs of Lancashire (although Briggs could be considered a Notts man, having been born in Sutton-in-Ashfield), Lohmann and Read from Surrey and Bates of Yorkshire. James Lillywhite accompanied the team as umpire, and on 18 September 1886 the party left Plymouth as first-class passengers aboard the Orient liner *Cuzco*.

Shaw and Shrewsbury's team to Australia, 1886–87. Left to right, standing:
W. Flowers, A. Shrewsbury, G. A. Lohmann, W. Gunn, W. Barnes, J. M. Read;
sitting, W. Bates, A. Shaw, J. Lillywhite, M. Sherwin, W. H. Scotton, R. G. Barlow;
front, J. Briggs.

In his amiable memoirs, R. G. Barlow gives us an insight into how the party spent their time on board. The voyage out was enlivened by several minstrel shows, in which Gunn made successful appearances as 'Tambourine'. (Sherwin was highly acclaimed for his performance as 'Bones'.) Gunn, Read, Sherwin and Barlow sang in the ship's Sunday Service choir, and with the addition of Scotton and Briggs formed a concert party which performed not only aboard ship but at various charity concerts arranged as the tour progressed. Among the repertoire were 'How Beautiful Upon the Mountains', 'Tell Me Shepherds', and 'When Other Lips'. The standbys of many a local choir, these songs no doubt anticipated the music that William's nephews, John and George, were in later years to sing and play. There were also ship sports. To nobody's surprise Mordecai Sherwin won the trial of strength, and William was an equally easy winner of the hop, step and jump, the long jump, and the hurdle race. The voyage ended on 29 October.

Unfortunately, on this his only tour of Australia, William Gunn did not greatly distinguish himself in the one way he would have wished – with the bat. Australian spectators never saw the best of Gunn, although Barlow recalls that his 'style of batting was very much admired out there'. But it was style rather than substance. If we leave aside his 150 out of a total of 803 made for Non-Smokers v Smokers, Gunn's average for the tour was a disappointing 21.53, his highest score being 61 not out against Melbourne's Australian XI. Yet he finished fourth in the averages, and Shrewsbury, who was top, managed only 34.64. No doubt the sheer demands made by the tour itinerary explain much of this. Nineteen hours on a train, followed by six hours on a boat and another ten hours of train travel is not conducive to mental or bodily freshness. For a man of Gunn's height, the hardships of such travel must have been especially difficult to resolve. But there can be no glossing over the disappointments, which were particularly acute in the two international matches, where he totalled a mere 23 runs from his four innings, and in which his major contribution seems to have been the unusual one of standing as umpire for part of the second match, even though he was playing for the England team.

We do not know how much Gunn earned from the tour, but Barlow was paid £320 and had all his expenses covered. Assuming that Gunn was similarly treated he certainly had no reason to complain. On the other hand the tour was long and exhausting, and the party arrived back in Plymouth on 7 May 1887, which allowed him no more than a fortnight before the next county season began.

If he was tired that summer, it did not greatly show. In the opening game against Surrey he scored 72 in the second innings, while none of his team-mates managed more than twenty in either. He followed this with 50 against Middlesex at Lord's, 78 against Lancashire at Trent Bridge and, on the same ground a fortnight later, 90 and 45 not out against Kent, thus being responsible for the bulk of the work that guaranteed Notts's victory. His finest performance that season, however, came in the return match against Sussex at Trent Bridge. Three Notts batsmen made over a century in the same innings; Barnes scored 120 and Shrewsbury 135. As for Gunn, his 205 not out was described by a Notts man as one of his greatest innings. 'He seldom, if ever, played better cricket,' C. H. Richards wrote, adding austerely, 'He displayed admirable defence, and at times hit hard and clean.' Which, considering that he batted for nearly seven and a half hours and hit nineteen fours, is perhaps unnecessarily cautious. He also scored a fine 61 for MCC v England in the MCC centenary week, the highest innings for his side.

The following season was, however, a grave disappointment, both for Notts and for Gunn himself. Shrewsbury was off in Australia, attending to the interests of the English football team, about which Ashley-Cooper offers the tight-lipped comment that Shrewsbury's explanations for going 'was not regarded as being quite adequate'. For the first time since 1864 the team lost more matches than it won. Gunn was never in form and although he played one or two fine innings – notably 69 against Surrey, 73 and 56 against Kent and 91 against the visiting Australians – he finished the season for Notts with an average of only 23.62.

His name, however, counted for a great deal. Even though his form was poor he was chosen for both Gentlemen–Players matches and was also a member of the England team for two of the three matches against the Australians. Sadly, he failed. In the First Test, played at Lord's, he batted at number nine and scored 2 and 8. In the Third Test, at Old Trafford, he moved up the order to number seven and scored 15. None of the games was remarkable for high scoring, yet Gunn must have been upset that for these important games he could not reverse his loss of form.

All great batsmen endure a period in their career when they cannot score runs. They are out to the one unplayable ball of the innings, or to a bad umpiring decision; a fielder brings off a near-impossible catch, or they are run out by a fluke throw. Then confidence begins to drain away, the ball goes to the field rather than through it, bowlers sense that they can add a famous name to their tally of victims. So it goes. So it went for Gunn in 1888. Perhaps he was simply tired. He was entitled to be. Since 1882 he had been playing sport without a break all the year round, either moving from cricket to football and back again, or, as in 1886–87, having virtually eighteen months of continuous cricket. It is significant that during the winter of 1888–89 he played only two matches for Notts County. Was he resting? If so, it paid off. In 1889 he enjoyed his greatest season to date.

He began with 74 against Sussex. In his next match, against Middlesex, he failed. Then came Surrey, the champions. It was a key fixture: the old lions versus the pretenders. Notts won by an innings and 153 runs and Gunn's innings of 118 – he was at the wicket for just over three and a half hours – was agreed by all who saw it to have been without blemish. 'A superb display of hitting and defence' the local newspaper crowed. After that there were runs against Lancashire (54), Derbyshire (78 and 50 not out), Kent (80) and Gloucestershire (61). Then came August and the weather turned sour. Up and down the country batsmen struggled. Even Gunn faltered. But he recovered and ended the season with a Notts average of 41.60. He was, by general consent, the best professional batsman of the year. Notts were once again first in the championship.

Gunn did not merely play outstanding cricket for his county that season. In the Gentlemen–Players match at the Oval he scored 61 and 98 not out. For North v South he scored 63 at Chichester and 57 not out at Hastings. His highest score was, however, at Lord's, for MCC v Northumberland. MCC batted first, with Gunn opening. He lost his partner when the score was nine, and was joined by Attewell. When play ended for the day the two were still together and the total had reached 325. The following day Attewell was finally out for 200 and MCC declared at 428 for 2. Gunn had scored 219 not out, including no fewer than 33 fours. After that, the 139 he scored for Shrewsbury's Notts XI against Scotland must have seemed fairly tame stuff.

Gunn was firmly established as one of the nation's great cricketers. The editor of *Wisden*, in speaking of him as the most successful batsman of 1889, said:

> We think we are correct in saying that no batsman of the same height has ever played in more elegant and perfect form. Certainly we know no professional at the present day whom it is a greater pleasure to watch. Even before he rose to his present fame as a batsman, Gunn was one of the most brilliant fields in the country, and it is the general opinion of practical cricketers that in the long field and at third man he has never had a superior.

His height certainly helped him. In his *Recollections and Reminiscences*, Lord Hawke remarks that when Gunn went into the sports outfitting business Johnny Briggs said to him, ' "I suppose he'll cut his old bats into two, and, with fresh handles, sell them to schoolboys or" – with a twinkle in his eye – "to Bobby Abel and myself" – both being decidedly short of stature.' But height alone cannot make a great batsman. Richard Daft noted that 'For so tall a man, [Gunn] is more elegant in his play than any man I have seen. From what I have heard by tradition, I should say that in much of his play he resembles a man whom he never saw – the great Fuller Pilch.'

All the commentators agree as to Gunn's elegance, which must have been produced by a combination of wrist and footwork. For so large a   45 man he was unusually quick on his feet. He was also of course immensely powerful. On more than one occasion he drove balls out of the ground, and a glance at the photograph taken of him at bat shows how high up he gripped the bat handle. He also had a very fine, very straight defensive technique. Several contemporaries, W. G. Grace among them, said that the only mystery about Gunn was that, having got himself in, he should ever allow himself to get out.

By the time the 1880s came to a close Gunn had achieved enough to make all those who had predicted great things of him feel well content. He was their champion. And, at the age of thirty-one, and at a time when great cricketers matured later and lasted longer than they do nowadays, it was quite possible to hope that the best was still to come.

3
THE GREAT PROFESSIONAL

During the winter of 1889–90 William Gunn played no football for Notts County. He may have been ill, but we have no record to tell us this was so, and it is probably safer to assume that he was no longer committed to football, at least as a professional player. Indeed, in September 1890 he was re-instated as an amateur. From now on his football was to be played at local level and on a casual basis. Yet his connections with Notts County were strengthened rather than weakened by his decision. In 1890 the club became a limited company and on 2 June that year Gunn was elected to the board of directors. He polled sixty-six votes, the fifth-highest number. No doubt his status had been enhanced by his deeds on the cricket field. That particular summer it could hardly have been otherwise.

The cricket season began with Shrewsbury and himself destroying the Sussex bowling at Trent Bridge. Their partnership of 398 was at that time a record partnership for first-class cricket. Shrewsbury took a shade under nine hours to score 267; Gunn's 196 took exactly six hours. It was an innings, Richards noted, 'worthy of the highest praise'. Sussex were crushed. So were Surrey, who came next, Gunn scoring 82 and 35. He slipped against Middlesex (14 and 20), recovered against Kent (45 run out), scored 46 in the return game against Sussex and 43 against the Australian tourists. On a difficult wicket at Sheffield he made 22 and 26 against Yorkshire, an innings vastly more important than the figures suggest. Notts won all these games. Then they began to falter and Gunn faltered with them. He finished the season with 833 runs for his county at an average of 34.71.

All this tells the less interesting half of the story. His representative cricket that summer makes for a far more extraordinary tale. It was not that he did particularly well for the Players, although his 44 against the Gentlemen at the Oval was a fine innings in trying conditions. But against

William Gunn and Arthur Shrewsbury, whose partnership of 398 for the second wicket against Sussex in 1890 remains the highest in Notts's history.

the Australians he performed with remarkable consistency. In the return Notts–Australians fixture he scored 47 out of 145 and 50 out of 138 in a match Notts won by 20 runs. He scored 31 and 30 not out against them for MCC. At Sheffield he made 43 for the Players of England. For England in the Tests he made 32 at the Oval (top score on a spiteful wicket) and at Lord's a crucial 34, again in very difficult conditions. England won both these very low-scoring games and on both occasions Gunn's batting was the chief difference between the two sides. At the end of the season, having scored 196 for MCC against Northumberland, who must have been sick of the sight of him, he scored 118 against the Australians, in a match held for the benefit of the Cricketers' Fund. By then the Australians must have been even more sick than Northumberland of the sight of Gunn coming out to bat.

Lord's that June was the venue for a match, Players of England v Australians, that has passed into cricketing history. The Players won the toss and chose to bat. Ulyett and Gunn opened and put on 66 before Ulyett was out. Barnes, Peel and Flowers all succeeded each other to the wicket, and stayed for varying lengths of time, and at the end of the day the score was 322 for 4, Gunn not out 147. At lunchtime the following day he was 193 not out, and he finally reached his second hundred just after three o'clock. According to a London newspaper reporter who was on the ground that day:

> Even then, though evidently very tired, he took no liberties, and it seemed a certainty that he would carry out his bat, when, to the general disappointment of the spectators, he played rather slackly at a ball from Lyons, and was bowled. He had been in while 516 runs were scored, and of this huge total his share was 228, the highest innings ever made against an Australian side in England . . . for nine hours and three-quarters he had met all the Australian bowlers with the same care and judgement, and a finer display of consistently watchful batting cannot be imagined.

It was an innings to draw out superlatives. Another correspondent, for a different newspaper, noted that:

> From any point of view this performance of Gunn's was remarkable in the highest degree. An innings of any length is rarely free from blemish of some sort or other, but, to the best of my knowledge . . . there was nothing that could be construed into a chance, and, indeed, the faulty strokes he made were of the fewest.

The Times commented as follows:

> Ten years have elapsed since Gunn first figured in the Nottinghamshire Eleven. When he first appeared at Lord's his style was so good that there were several old cricketers who foretold a big future for him. These predictions have been fulfilled.

Punch attempted some verses.

> Such calm, graceful batting, of funk so defiant,
>   As proof against flurry, deserved the crowd's roar,
> 'Twas cricket indeed, when the Nottingham Giant,
>   Against the best bowling, piled up that huge score;
> And the crowds as they watched him smite, play, block or run,
> Could grasp the full meaning of 'Sure as a Gunn'.

The MCC marked his great achievement by presenting him with a silver cup.

◆ ● ◆

9 Hope Drive, The Park.

Gunn was no doubt pleased when the season came to an end. He could now afford to take life easily. His business was prospering. He, his wife and baby daughter, who had been born in 1889, were thus able to move to 9 Hope Drive, The Park. The Park was and is an exclusive residential area near to Nottingham's city centre, remarkable for the grand houses that were mostly erected in the latter half of the nineteenth century by a local architect of national reputation, T. C. Hine. They were bought by captains of industry and commerce, who lived and entertained amid scenes of considerable affluence. Many of the houses indeed contained full-size ballrooms. William Gunn's house did not run to that, but it was a substantial residence and a far cry from the two-up, two-down of his boyhood. The new house was further proof of his success and of his pride in his reputation both as sportsman and businessman. He was now a public figure, eagerly sought after for civic functions. That winter he busied himself with his business and domestic affairs and made occasional appearances at banquets and concerts.

◆◆◆

William Gunn, businessman. A letter to a client of Gunn & Moore, 1893.

His new life style did not however take away his appetite for cricket. Among his notable scores during the summer of 1891 were 161 against Sussex at Brighton, 109 against Kent, made 'by the most superb and finished batting', and 169 for Players v Gentlemen at Hastings. It should here be noted that Gunn and Shrewsbury so regularly scored hundreds against Sussex that it was said that when Notts played at Brighton and won the toss the rest of the side would disappear to the beach. He finished the season with 40 and 62 not out for a Notts XI against the Gentlemen of England at Scarborough.

The following season was one of more modest achievement, although the cricket during his 58 against Surrey at the Oval, when he shared in a match-winning stand with Barnes, was said by *Wisden* to be 'the finest seen in London during the season'. That winter he played his last-ever games for Notts County.

The 1893 summer saw him at his peak. His final figures – 1,330 runs for Notts at an average of 44.33 and overall 2,057 runs at 42.85 – were the best of any batsman in the country. Stoddart's aggregate was higher but his average was lower. Gunn scored five centuries for his county: 120 against Middlesex, 109 against Sussex and 156 in the return match at Brighton, 150 against Yorkshire at Bradford and 129 against Kent. Add to this many other major scores, including a 90 and a 74, and he can claim to have done more than his share for Notts that season. Sadly, however, the once-great team were on the wane. The reason lay not in the batting but in the bowling. The incomparable Alfred Shaw had been allowed to go – long before his time, many muttered. Attewell continued to take wickets, but they cost him dear; and there were no other class bowlers to call on. As we shall see, a new era of great Notts bowlers was about to dawn, and one of them would be a Gunn. But for the moment Notts cricket was betwixt and between. Which may explain why William Gunn, after a lapse of so many years, was once again called upon to bowl. In all he sent down 38 overs that summer, and took four wickets at a cost of 127 runs. And in each succeeding season of the 1890s he would bowl a little, and take a few wickets for a good many runs.

However, it was his batting that counted. Quite apart from his performances for Notts, Gunn scored 124 for MCC against Sussex at Lord's, and 64 for an Eleven of England against the Australians at Trent Bridge. (This game, which was played on 26, 27 and 28 June, was for Shrewsbury's benefit, and the England side, led by WG himself, won by an innings and 153 runs. The match benefited Shrewsbury by £600.)

The 1893 England team to play Australia at Lord's, captained by Stoddart in place of Grace who had broken his finger. Left to right, standing: E. Wainwright, A. Mold, W. Gunn, J. M. Read; sitting, R. Peel, A. E. Stoddart, W. G. Grace, W. H. Lockwood, A. Shrewsbury; front, G. MacGregor, F. S. Jackson, W. Flowers.

❖ ❖ ❖

That summer Gunn inevitably played in the three Tests against Australia. In the drawn game at Lord's he scored 2 and 77, made only 16 in the game at the Oval which England won by an innings, and at Old Trafford, where there was again a draw, he scored 102 not out and 11.

By comparison, 1894 was a disappointment. Ill-health meant that Gunn did not play for Notts until the end of June when, although hardly match-fit and undoubtedly short of practice, he nevertheless did well enough to finish top of the county averages. His two centuries against Somerset, 121 not out and 101, were high points. It was not enough to prevent the Notts decline from continuing, and it became even steeper in 1895. Once again Gunn appears not to have been in full health, and as a

William Gunn as a director of Notts County. Left to right, standing: T. E. Harris (sec), J. Chadburn, S. Donnelly, W. Gunn, F. Fletcher, E. Allsop, J. Goode (trainer); sitting, J. Hendry, A. Shelton, C. Bramley, D. Calderhead (capt), D. Bruce, A. E. Harrison, I. Stothern.

result was absent from several key games. Nevertheless he scored 111 against Leicestershire and a magnificent 219 in four hours 55 minutes in a Notts total of 726 against Sussex.

In 1896 matters began to mend. Gunn was in better health and so was Arthur Shrewsbury, who had been absent for much of the previous two seasons but now seemed entirely restored. The nature of his illness has never been explained but it seems almost certain to have been nervous, whereas Gunn's was certainly physical and no doubt came about from the great strain he put on himself during those exhausting years when he had been switching continually from cricket to football and back again. Now, although he was absent from four matches because of ill-health, he was more or less fit, and Notts rose from twelfth to sixth position in the table. His more important innings of the summer included 135 against Derbyshire and, in the return against the same county, 207 not out, which was described in a newspaper of the day as 'as near perfection as it would be possible to attain'. He also scored 138 for MCC against Sussex and for MCC and Ground made 39 against the Australians at Lord's.

That summer there were the usual Test matches between the two countries. In the first match, at Lord's, Gunn scored 25 and 13 not out. He was not in the team that played at Old Trafford, presumably because of ill-health, but was chosen to play at the Oval. However, Lohmann, Abel, Richardson, Hayward and himself were dissatisfied with the £10 offered them for the match and demanded £20. The Surrey committee turned down their request, and Lohmann and Gunn did not play. In the event their absence was not important. England scored 145 and 84 and bowled out Australia for 119 and 44. But the principle was what mattered. The men can scarcely be criticized for asking for more. They were professionals, huge crowds came to watch them, and Test matches guaranteed a great deal of money for the counties that staged them. Why should not the players receive adequate compensation for their efforts? Gunn was not a greedy man. We have seen that by this stage in his career he did not need the money. What he did expect was proper recognition of his worth. If that was not forthcoming then he would not play. It was not and he did not.

In 1897 Notts dropped back to tenth position in the county table. Gunn, however, was in imperious form. Perhaps his number of outstanding innings had something to do with the fact that it was the year in which he was granted a benefit match. Perhaps he wanted to show that the English team did without him at its peril. Whatever the reason, or reasons, his performances that year were exceptional, even by his standards. The innings that pleased most people was the 125 he scored against Surrey on the Whit-Monday of his benefit match. Rain spoilt the match, but nothing could spoil the crowd's enthusiasm for Gunn's masterly performance with the bat. His backplay against Richardson was, so Ashley-Cooper assures us, 'the outstanding feature of his innings'.

That season he also scored 110 against Yorkshire at Trent Bridge, 152 against Derbyshire on the Derby ground and in the return match a massive 230. Not surprisingly he topped the county's averages.

The following year, 1898, it was Shrewsbury's turn to come top. Yet Gunn's form was even better than it had been in 1897. Then he had scored 1,010 runs for an average of 45.90. Now he amassed 1,115 runs, average 46.46. His 125 at Brighton against Sussex involved him in a stand of 241 with Shrewsbury, while at the Oval, in just under eight hours, he finished with 236 not out (it included a six, twenty-four fours and a five). As with so many of his long innings he gave no chance and made virtually no mistake, and when it was all over he was called to the front of the pavilion where the large crowd gave him a prolonged ovation.

Judging from this and similar innings it seems that when the mood was on him Gunn was quite simply impregnable. No matter what the bowling or conditions, he would bat with the kind of flawless, unruffled assurance that is given only to the greatest masters. An odd fact about these long innings was that they rarely increased in tempo as they went on. There were of course occasions on which Gunn could score at speed. Indeed, in that same season – 1898 – he scored 139 in four hours for the Players at Lord's in the match arranged for W. G. Grace's birthday; and at Scarborough he hit an even faster 137 for C. I. Thornton's XI v Yorkshire. But there were clearly other occasions when he made up his mind not to get out. Nothing would therefore deflect him from his purpose of occupying the crease. It was not that he was slow or improperly cautious on such occasions. When all is said and done, 236 in eight hours can hardly be called slow batting. But it was as though from first to last every ball was to be treated as it deserved, and no ball would be allowed to outwit him. At the end of his historic 228 against the Australians only tiredness got the better of him. Against Surrey at the Oval not even fatigue it seemed could disturb his presence of mind, his singleness of purpose.

The following year, for the first time in the decade, he dropped below second in the Notts averages. This time he finished third, behind Shrewsbury (who else?) and A. O. Jones. Even so, he scored 1,230 runs at an average of 45.56, which goes to show just how strong the Notts batting was. His best performances were 150 v Sussex at Brighton and 116 against Lancashire. He also scored 90 v Derbyshire at Trent Bridge and exactly the same number of runs in the return at Derby; 57 in the return game against Sussex; 68 at the Oval against Surrey; 52 and 54 against Gloucestershire at Trent Bridge; 55 not out against Kent at Catford; 50 against Yorkshire at Bradford; and 72 against Middlesex at Trent Bridge.

On 1, 2, 3 June Australia came to Trent Bridge for a Test match.

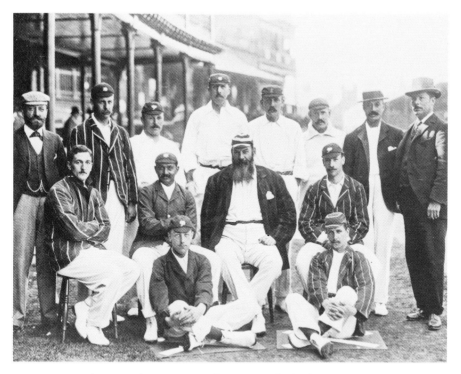

England v Australia at Trent Bridge, 1899 – the final Test appearances of W. G. Grace and William Gunn. Left to right, standing: R. G. Barlow (umpire), T. W. Hayward, G. H. Hirst, W. Gunn, J. T. Hearne, W. Storer, W. Brockwell (twelfth man), V. A. Titchmarsh (umpire); sitting, C. B. Fry, K. S. Ranjitsinhji, W. G. Grace, F. S. Jackson; front, W. Rhodes, J. T. Tyldesley.

England's 'is a splendid team', the *Pall Mall Gazette* wrote, 'even including Gunn, whose place we fear is more a compliment to the Notts County Committee than to any form that player has shown this season.' Since Gunn had played in only three county games until then, and had scored 55 not out in one of them, this seems an uncalled-for remark. Perhaps the *Gazette* thought as much, for it goes on: 'Still, Gunn is so capable of rising to the occasion that we should not be surprised to see him come off best of any batsmen in the side.' Sadly, it was not to be. In England's first innings he was bowled by Jones for 14. Admittedly that was fifth-highest score (Fry made 50, Ranji 42, both very luckily, W.G. 28 and J. T. Tyldesley 22), but it can hardly have been to the liking of the large crowd that packed into Trent Bridge. In the second innings Jones bowled him for 3. It was his last Test. That it was W. G. Grace's last Test also (he was out for 1) does not lessen the sadness of the occasion, although there is perhaps a certain fitness in the fact that the greatest cricketer of his and perhaps any other age and the great professional should have ended their international careers at the same time.

So the 1890s came to an end. For no fewer than five seasons, those of 1891, 1893, 1894, 1896 and 1897, Gunn had topped the batting averages of a county whose strength in batting was acknowledged to be second to none. For another four years he had been second. Only in 1899 had he fallen as low as third. During that same period he had played dozens of important innings for the Players and other representative teams. For MCC he had regularly scored hundreds, often against the fiercest opposition. And in at least two Test series he had been the mainstay of the English batting, and sometimes the match-winner. He had become a much-respected director of the football club for whom he had played with great distinction. And his business was flourishing to such an extent that Gunn & Moore's bats were now regularly supplied to leading batsmen the world over. C. B. Fry, Ranji, Victor Trumper, Jessop, even the great Doctor himself, all used and swore by the bats that William Sherwin crafted and for which he took sole responsibility.

How much longer would William Gunn go on playing cricket? He was now turned forty and the years were beginning to exact some revenge for the stresses to which he had subjected his physique. It would be only natural to suppose that the fierce flame of ambition that had sustained him for so long was beginning to die a little. Still, he was not yet done. And besides, there was now playing for Notts another Gunn whom he must nurse along a little.

4

MORE GUNNS

In 1874 John Gunn, William's elder brother, had married Jane Richmond, a girl some five years his senior. In the family Bible, which is now in the possession of Peter Townsend, her date of birth is given as 27 August 1844 and her parents' names as Elizabeth and John Richmond. These bare facts apart, we know nothing about her, although it is possible that some cricketing blood ran in her veins. In any event, we have been told that she was a distant relative of T. L. 'Tich' Richmond, that most idiosyncratic of Notts cricketers, who played once and once only for England and was reputedly the worst fielder of his time.

On their marriage the couple moved out to Hucknall Torkyard. Hucknall, as it is now called, is today part of the sprawling Nottingham conurbation, but in the 1870s it was a small, sleepy village. It had, however, known a moment of fame. In 1824 the bones of Lord Byron were brought back from Greece and, amid scenes of great pomp, laid to rest in the parish churchyard. No pomp surrounded the arrival of the Gunns. They set up a fish and greengrocery business in the Portland Road and it was there, on 19 July 1876, that a first son, John Richmond Gunn, was born. Nearly three years later, on 13 June 1879, a second son arrived. He was named, simply, George. It is good to think that one small and apparently undistinguished village should have become the final resting place of a great, devil-may-care poet, and the birthplace of an equally great, devil-may-care batsman.

Unlike Byron, however, the young Gunns had no silver spoon with which to sup their gruel. The business at Hucknall cannot have prospered, for in the year that William Gunn began to establish his place in the county team his brother brought Jane and the two boys into the city. They now took a house and a shop in Lenton and it was here that their father introduced John and George to cricket. Although by no means a rival to his brother, John Gunn was a competent club cricketer, and his elder son recalls going to see him play for Lenton United. 'My job was at   59 that time to score for the team as well as I could,' he says in a scrap of unpublished memoir (on which we shall often draw), although 'being so young' it is unlikely he would have done the job unaided. He also says that his father would sometimes take him to see his Uncle William play. However, the demands of the shop were such that those occasions were few and far between.

The boys' earliest education was at Lenton Trust Holy Trinity National (Infants) School, Church Street, Old Lenton, directly opposite the church itself. Here were:

Teachers, Miss Agnes Mace, Headmistress
Also W. Whitwell, Miss E. Wood and Miss A. Marshall
Size of School – Large Room – 30 × 30 ft, ht 29 ft, for 112 children
Two other classrooms 18 × 20 ft, ht 18 ft for 45 children
17 × 17 ft, ht 18 ft for 38 children

On 6 April 1883 the infant school records list a number of children as 'transferred who will be seven before the next examination. Four children passed the examination.' John Richmond Gunn was not among the lucky four. He was however transferred to the boys' junior school, and on the same day the put-upon headmaster of the juniors writes: 'admitted twenty boys this week, eighteen from the infants school. Of this number, some seven or eight could not say all their letters: expect to find them a drawback for the whole year.' Whether John was to prove a drawback to his contemporaries we have no way of knowing, but his fragment of autobiography reveals that he never had more than an amiable nodding acquaintance with the rules of grammar and orthography.

Presumably George moved up some three years later, although there is no record of his having done so. But the records for 1886 are understandably scanty. They record merely that a number of children were transferred on 8 March, when their teacher, Miss Docherty, became seriously ill. A month later she was dead of typhoid fever.

According to John Gunn's memoir, when he was seven the family moved the short distance from Lenton to Hyson Green. Yet we can find no record in *Wright's Directory* for Nottingham for 1883 that the Gunns were at 56 Radford Road, Hyson Green, which John gives as their address, and which certainly was their home in 1887. We can only assume that when he came to write his autobiography his memory occasionally let him down. What is undisputed is the fact that 1887 was

56 Radford Road, as it is today.

❦ ● ❧

the year of his father's death, and it left Jane to carry on the fishmonger's business on her own. No doubt the boys helped. But for them there were other attractions.

Radford Road was, as it still is, mostly taken up with a long string of shops which served the Hyson Green community. It is also hard by an enormous expanse of parkland called the Forest which, together with the Meadows, made up in the last decades of the nineteenth century the largest area for cricket and football in the whole of Nottingham. Literally hundreds of teams played their matches on the Forest, and it was here that John and George would go, whenever they had a free moment: to watch, to cheer, to support their local favourites, and most of all to play.

And play. For it was here, during long and arduous hours of practice, that they began to develop those skills which were to make them two of the great cricketers of their age. In his memoir John writes that:

George and myself used to be on the Forest at 5.30 am with our coats up for a wicketkeeper, toss who was to bat and sometimes one of us would be batting for two or three days, but we had to bowl each other out. When we could not manage to get to the Forest we used to play in the passage, or against Daft's wall in Belper Road, where we often broke a few windows, which of course my Mother had to pay for, 'it was always those Gunn boys' who did the damage, even if some other boys were responsible.

The passage to which John refers is still there, and its furthest end is a blocking post which no doubt made a suitable wicket. As for 'Daft's wall': the Daft in question was William Daft, whose address is given in *Wright's Directory* as 60 Radford Road, and who lists his profession as 'Butcher'. It would be lovely to think that he had some family connection with the great Richard Daft, who had done so much to introduce the boys' uncle to the first-class game. Unfortunately, we have come across no evidence to support such an assumption.

The boys were evidently cricket-mad. Not only did they get up at the crack of dawn to start their single-wicket matches, they also played every lunchtime and evening. One old gentleman who regularly passed them as he took his evening constitutional told them that with their diligence they were certain one day to play cricket for England. Events were to prove him right, but the days of greatness lay far ahead. In the meantime it was practise, practise, practise, and then more practise. Presumably George must have had the harder time of it. Younger than his brother, physically ailing, he no doubt spent a disproportionate amount of time bowling at John.

At some point the boys changed school, although we do not know exactly when or for where. We assume that their new school was the Berridge Road School at Hyson Green, which had opened in 1884 and which was conveniently close to their home. They are not mentioned in school reports, but that does not mean a great deal. The only boys whose names appear do so because they were spectacularly dirty, more than usually badly dressed, diseased, without money, or regularly absent. It is, however, slightly odd that cricket does not feature in the school reports, if only because the head teacher records that on race days 'attendance was sparse', and it is at least as likely that attendance would have been sparse on the days of big cricket matches, especially since two of the pupils could
claim a close family link with the hero of Nottinghamshire, William

The 'wicket' used by John and George at the entrance to the Forest.

John Gunn aged 11.

Gunn. For, as we have seen, as the 1880s progressed so, rapidly, did William's career. Besides, at least one of the teachers played cricket. In his memoir John recalls seeing Mr W. King playing for the School Board team on the Forest. 'Not a bad player either,' he comments.

He would not have had a great deal of time for watching, however. When he was not at school or playing with his younger brother he was singing in the Christchurch Choir, New Radford and – bringing his two great loves together – playing cricket for the church choir team. 'A gentleman named Trevelyan Ward used to give us a shilling for every twenty runs we made when playing in Saturday matches, of course we did try, and often I would make my week's spending money.' And there, in those schoolboy games, we catch our first glimmerings of a cricketing career.

The glimmerings were soon to grow stronger. In common with the vast majority of boys of his time, John left school at the age of fourteen. He was put to work in the lace firm of Radford and Cutts, or, as he tells it, 'after finishing with Christchurch I joined the Radford and Cutt's team where I worked as a boy in the draughting room.' It is worth noting that in this account the firm's cricket team comes before its business. And for John at least, it undoubtedly did. He was at Radford and Cutts for six years, but 'not meaning to go in for that game', as he puts it, he would 'go and ask Mr John Cutts if I could go down to Beeston, to practise, this was in the long room at the "Boat Inn" in those days and it was quite a treat for me to get away from the Draughting Room, to the job I had set my heart on doing, but one day when I asked to go to practise John Cutts asked me what it was going to be, cricket or draughting? and I was most delighted when given leave to go in for cricket.'

He had obviously compressed a good deal into that short account, but it is clear that he was not the stuff of which a dedicated workman could be made – not unless the work in question was cricket. And here there can be no doubt of his dedication. When he was not practising it was because he was playing for the Radford and Cutts team, as he regularly did. Then, 'Notts Castle asked me if I would play for them.' And now he is on his way. For as we have seen the highly prestigious Notts Castle club had close connections with the county; and John himself recalls that the secretary Henry Turner 'found I could play a little, and introduced me to the County people.' No doubt that is true, but it is unlikely to have been the whole truth. John Gunn was, after all, the nephew of the great William, and although their uncle did not see much of the boys when they were young, it is clear that his interest in them was sharpened when he began to realize that they, too, were unusually gifted and promising cricketers. Moreover, William still turned out for the Notts Castle team when his other commitments allowed, and he would thus have had a chance to see his nephew's progress at close quarters.

That progress was sound enough for John to be included in the team of twenty-two colts who played the county XI at Trent Bridge on Easter Monday and Tuesday, 6 and 7 April, 1896. He did not impress with the bat, making nine in each innings. His bowling, however, was a different matter. In the county team's first innings he bowled six overs and finished with three wickets for four runs. In his brief comment on the match, Richards remarks that 'None of the Colts gave any promise of exceptional ability as batsmen.' On the other hand, 'in the bowling department . . . J. Gunn, a nephew of Wm Gunn, and T. Wass, made a distinctly favourable impression.' Which is hardly surprising, since John and 'Topsy' Wass were to become two of the finest bowlers of their age.

John's next match was for the county colts against Yorkshire Colts. The game was played at Worksop on 4 and 5 May, and as far as John was concerned it was a dismal failure. He scored 0 and 9, and took one wicket for 15 runs in five overs. Nor did he do much better in his next game: for Professionals of the County v. Amateurs of the County, the match being played at Trent Bridge on 11 and 12 May. The Amateurs scored 398 in their only innings (Mr R. P. Daft 110; J. Gunn 14 overs, 19 runs, no wickets) and in reply the Professionals, who were without William Gunn, managed 161 in their first innings (J. Gunn 5) and at the second attempt reached 172 for 4 (J. Gunn did not bat).

Scarcely more auspicious a start than his uncle had made some sixteen years previously. Yet the county committee kept faith. It had, after all, paid handsome dividends in the case of William Gunn. And so on 13 and 14 August 1896, John Gunn was chosen to play his first county game for a much weakened Notts side (they were without William Gunn, Dixon and Shrewsbury) against Gloucestershire at Bristol. Gloucestershire batted first and scored 196. Attewell took four wickets for 40 runs in 30 overs. John Gunn did not bowl at all and in the Notts first innings he batted at number ten and made 12 not out. In their second innings Gloucestershire scored 262 (Jessop 71) and again John did not bowl. His misery must have been complete when Notts were dismissed for a mere 52 and he was out without scoring. Only one occurrence at Bristol can have given him any satisfaction and, bearing in mind his love of poring over *Wisden* in his old age, it is more than likely that he returned to the record of his first-ever county match and took relish from a particular detail of Gloucestershire's second innings: Dr W. G. Grace c Gunn b Jones 1.

Nor at the time did his modest triumph go unremarked. William sent him a congratulatory telegram from his sickbed, and in his memoir John recalls that 'It was a feather in my cap, to bag W.G. in my first game for the County. From that time,' he adds, 'my heart was set on the game.' Catching the great doctor in the deep-field was John Gunn's most notable achievement in 1896. Indeed, if we leave aside the promise of his brief bowling spell for the colts at Easter, it was his *only* achievement. He clearly had much to do and a long way to go before he could come within range of his uncle's prowess.

At the end of the season a matter came up that was to be of great importance for John Gunn and for all young Notts cricketers. The county committee's report for 1896 contained the following paragraph:

> Your committee are deeply impressed with the necessity of establishing a system by which the most promising of the rising players may be retained in the County and their ability developed. Now that the Club has been so happily freed from debt, a scheme has been proposed for this purpose . . . It is earnestly hoped that such a scheme, if adopted, may be the means in the course of time, of so strongly recruiting the County team as to cause it to take its place once more in the very front rank of English Counties.

What this conceals is the committee's very real fear that young players were being lost to the county because of the refusal of older ones to stand aside (a refusal that required them to perform with some consistency and to be able to count on the support of county members) and the added fear that this was proving to have unfortunate results. For Notts were no longer the force that they had been. Since 1892, when they finished second in the table, they had done badly in the Inter-County Contests, as they were called, finishing sixth out of nine in 1893, seventh out of nine in 1894, twelfth out of fourteen in 1895 and sixth in 1896. As has been noted, the bowling was very weak. Clearly, something had to be done. In 1897 the committee were able to announce that among those engaged on the groundstaff was J. Gunn. They also announced that they had obtained as coach Mr W. Marshall, 'an old and experienced cricketer, with every knowledge of the game in all its bearings,' and they were optimistic 'that under his able supervision the young professionals will derive great benefit.'

In 1897 Walter Marshall was forty-two years old. He had played in virtually every Notts Castle match for many seasons, he was much admired as a cricketer and tactician, had sound theories about how the game should be played and worked hard and expected others to do the same. He was a martinet. John's son Eric remembers how, as a very small boy, he and others were recruited by the great Walter to walk the length and breadth of the ground at Trent Bridge, picking up every daisy, matchstick and piece of paper they could see. In his memoir John recalls without much love his early days on the groundstaff.

> We had to bowl at all the team members who came for practice, and often I would not finish till 7.0 pm and my feet were very sore, mind you after your first season or two your feet became very hard. We had a Mr

◆ ● ◆

The Notts groundstaff for 1901 with their autocratic coach, Walter Marshall, who joined the staff in 1897 at the same time as John Gunn. Left to right, standing: T. G. Wass, J. Atkinson, J. Iremonger, W. Ross, P. Harrison; sitting, C. Pepper, C. E. Dench, P. Mason, W. Marshall, G. Anthony, A. W. Hallam, J. Gunn; front, A. Maurer, I. M. Harrison.

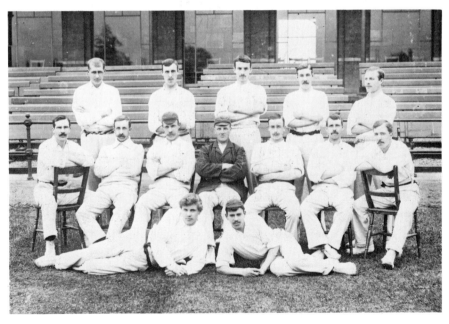

Walter Marshall as coach, he would keep us bowling at the nets all day long, then we should perhaps have a County game the next day, very often I used to feel tired before we started the match after all that bowling, at the time we had run short of bowlers all at once and Tom Wass and myself were doing most of it, I was very pleased when one of the committee noticed this, and gave me orders to bowl only when I felt like it.

Yet if it was a hard grounding it undoubtedly did much to help him develop that phenomenal accuracy and stamina that were essential components of his bowling skills. Of course, he was a strong, well-built man, on the short side perhaps and in later life inclined first to stockiness and later to a more generous body spread. But in his prime he was physically very fit and surprisingly fleet of foot. Eric recalls his father, on an occasion when he was well past his fiftieth birthday, outstripping his sons in a race for a bus; and he also remembers him, in a fit of temper, when Eric was courting and had arrived home late one night, picking up the young man's bicycle and throwing it the length of the garden.

The training John Gunn received under Walter Marshall, coupled with those years of painstaking practice with his younger brother, meant that he soon began to realise his potential. And no doubt the many hours he spent bowling at committee members and fellow cricketers had much to do with his honing of run-up and delivery. For his high, left-arm action was a model of economy. Speaking of a later period, Willis Walker recalled that 'Three short strides and that was it. He bowled an over more quickly than anyone else I ever came across. If it was a maiden you hadn't the time to draw breath before the ball was back at the other end.' Of course, John was slower by the time Willis Walker saw him in action. But even at his quickest he did not use a long run-up.

Nor was it bowling alone at which he began to excel. He was soon known and feared as an outstanding fielder, especially at cover point. Ashley-Cooper wrote of him that 'always paying the closest attention to the game, he seems able to anticipate a batsman's strokes with the result being that he has always been regarded as a fieldsman with whom it would be folly to take a liberty.' And as for his batting, that also developed fast. In 1897 he scored 107 for Notts against the Philadelphians and finished with an average of 23.22

Yet his greatest triumph of that season was undoubtedly with the ball. It came in the game against Yorkshire, played at Dewsbury on 15, 16 and 17 July. Notts batted first and scored 260. In reply Yorkshire managed only 139 and John Gunn's figures read: 18.2 overs, 13 maidens, 22 runs, 6 wickets. Yorkshire therefore followed on (the permitted margin at that time was 120 runs) and in their second innings did a great deal better, scoring 358. John did not repeat his devastating bowling of the first innings, but finished with the best figures: four wickets for 114 runs from forty-seven overs. As matters turned out Yorkshire then nearly won. The wicket turned nasty and Notts in their second innings finished on 151 for 8. They were saved by a masterly innings from William Gunn, who was 86 not out when the game ended.

Two of the great Gunns were therefore in action together. By all accounts William's innings was out of the ordinary, but by then the extraordinary was expected of him. What of his nephew's bowling? Richards, that master of sedate understatement, remarked that the Yorkshire batsmen 'were unable to cope'. A less restrained response came from a Notts supporter who was on the ground to see John's first great performance. As John himself recalled in his memoir: 'Every time I took a wicket a pigeon flew into the air, it appears a Nottingham man on the ground was sending them back to Nottingham. When I took my sixth wicket a voice was heard shouting "no more pigeons left Jack". He was a real Notts supporter.' To which could be added that the man had seen some greatness and should know it.

The year 1897 thus marked John Gunn's arrival as a genuine force in cricket. It was also a time of great personal change. On 8 September his mother died. Since his father's death she had been carrying on the family business, initially with the help of both sons and then with George's alone. For John had moved. Having briefly lived at 58 Bridlington Street, he was now lodging at 4 Bathley Street with William's sisters, as a newly married man. William's family had moved there from Kirk White Street in 1882. Bathley Street was within hailing distance of Trent Bridge, and for the rest of his long life John Gunn was always to live close to his beloved ground. His wife, Grace, was the daughter of a Tom Knowles, who worked in a lace factory at Radford, as had his daughter before her marriage.

Early in 1896 the couple had their first child, a son to whom they gave the names John William. There were to be other children. Cyril was born in 1898, Connie in 1899 and Eric in 1906. In the meantime there was much cricket to be played and a living to be earned.

5
UNCLE AND NEPHEW

William Gunn must have watched with a good deal of pride his nephew's rapid progress. Eric Gunn has told us that his father before establishing himself in the Notts side had wondered whether to join Werneth, for the league club had made him an attractive offer. His uncle, however, would not hear of it. John was to play for his native county. William thus became something of a surrogate father to John and to George: encouraging, advising and, as we shall see, helping them in more material ways. They were the sons for whom he and his wife no doubt yearned. They were to follow in his footsteps. Which meant that John Gunn was to play for Notts and play with distinction. He soon began to do so.

In the summer of 1898 he took part in fifteen matches for the county. He scored 183 runs at an average of 15.25 and his best innings was the 47 he made against Surrey at the Oval, on the occasion of his uncle's 236. As for bowling, he sent down 353 overs and took 25 wickets for 769 runs. His average was 30.76 and his best performance was the eight for 108 he took against Yorkshire's strong batting, during the course of which he bowled no fewer than 66 overs, an effort which tired even him. As late as 1953, writing to a young admirer in New Zealand, he remarked that he had found that particular spell 'rather hard work'.

The following summer he played in seventeen matches. As a batsman he went to the wicket twenty-four times, scored 327 runs, with a best innings of 60 against Lancashire, and finished with an average of 17.21. It was a slight improvement on the previous year. In bowling, however, he advanced much more rapidly. In county matches alone he finished top of the Notts averages, claiming 56 wickets from 584 overs at an average of 23.04. In all matches he finished second, just behind Topsy Wass, although he still had the largest number of wickets for any Notts bowler that season. Among several notable performances were five for 39 against Lancashire, four for 20 against Derbyshire and, most spectacular of all, against Middlesex at Lord's, five for 50 in the first innings and then, in the second, when Middlesex needed a mere 120 to win, five for 16, including 'Plum' Warner for nought and a hat-trick at the expense of Hayman, Ford and Rawlin. Notts won the match by 52 runs. One other of his bowling feats that season deserves remembering. Against Sussex he took five for 87, including Murdoch bowled for 2 and Ranji caught-and-bowled for 178. It was perhaps this innings that caused John to tell his young New Zealand correspondent that 'you don't see any players now like Ranji and Fry, a nice pair to bowl at when they got going. I have [had] some hours at them both, I should say that Ranji was the best player I have ever seen, such quick eyes and supple wrists.'

A good season for John Gunn, then, but a poor one for the county. They finished tenth and the reason is not far to seek. Gunn and Wass had to do most of the bowling. It is therefore not surprising that before the summer was over both of them began to flag. Gunn indeed strained his side and bowled comparatively little towards the season's end. Attewell it is true bowled 451 overs, but he took only nineteen wickets and was clearly at the end of his long and distinguished career. A. O. Jones had some good spells. But when all is said and done it was the newcomers who had to shoulder the main burden.

The end of the season therefore brought welcome relief. How did John Gunn spend the winter? He played local football, at which he was good enough to feature in Second XI games for Nottingham Forest. He sang in local choirs. Like his uncle, he had a good singing voice – in his case it was a light, sure-pitched baritone. Since in those days a major form of entertainment was provided by the many choirs that were formed out of church and community, and which performed at concerts and for charitable occasions, it is hardly surprising that John, a former chorister, should have joined the choir of All Hallows Church, West Bridgford, from which grew the Lady Bay male voice choir, of which more will be heard presently.

What of finances? The county club paid him a retainer, presumably Forest provided a little bootmoney; and his uncle no doubt found him odd work connected with Gunn & Moore. One way and another it was not difficult to survive, even with a wife and growing family. Neighbours and acquaintances recall John as an easy-going man who did not greatly bother his head about money. So long as there was enough for meals, for an occasional pipe and a pint, there was not much to worry about. That winter of 1899–1900 he would also have watched with interest the major alterations taking place at Trent Bridge. The success of the Test match of the previous summer had encouraged the county committee to bid for regular Test cricket. They expanded accommodation, so that the ground would in future hold between 20,000 and 25,000 spectators, enlarged the pavilion, improved facilities and installed a new practice-room. The entire work cost £4,000 and by the end of the winter all was ready. So was John Gunn.

In July 1900 Richard Daft died. An era had closed. But another was opening, for 1900 was the year in which John Gunn gave notice of powers beyond the ordinary. In all, he played 19 matches for Notts. His batting was still no more than competent, but it was increasingly reliable, as the figures show. He scored 557 runs at an average of 24.22, including a highest innings of 70 and several other useful scores. For example he made 55 against Yorkshire and 55 not out against MCC and Ground. By all accounts he was at this stage of his career a slow scorer, but he was developing a tough, pragmatic style of batting that would serve him admirably in the coming years. Left-handed, compact, quick on his feet and with very strong wrists, bowlers were beginning to find him something of a nuisance. Which is the least that opposing batsmen must have thought of him. That season he finished with 90 wickets, at an average of 21.39. In all he bowled the large number of 714 overs, and on no fewer than seven occasions took five wickets or more in an innings. In the county he was becoming much talked about, and his reputation was spreading beyond its borders. That summer he had his first taste of representative cricket, notably for North v South. Another Gunn was beginning to make a stir at national level.

There is no doubt that John Gunn's tremendous advance as a bowler had a great deal to do with the presence in the Notts side of Tom (Topsy) Wass. It is an old and true saying that bowlers hunt in pairs, and Notts now had a formidable pair of opening bowlers. In his memoir John recalls Henry Turner, who had become the club's secretary in 1895, saying to him that 'It's a good job you and Tom Wass have come out bowlers' – the reason being, John adds, that there were so many of the county's bowlers retiring at about that time. 1900, indeed, saw the last of Attewell. Great servant of the club though he had been, his absence was not to be missed. Gunn and Wass had been toughened by the previous summer. They were now match-hardened, capable of prolonged spells of bowling – and they loved their work.

Like all outstanding pairs of bowlers, they contrasted with and so complemented each other. Tom Wass bowled right-handed, with a high, side-on action. He was fast to fast-medium, powerfully built, tall, mature. He had been born in 1873 and was therefore twenty-six in the summer of 1900, a surprisingly late age for a bowler to come good. But it meant that by the time he became a regular member of the Notts side Wass had largely mastered his craft. For the most part he bowled straight, but had a devastating leg-break which he could bowl at full pace. In his memoir John goes so far as to say that he regarded Tom Wass as the greatest bowler he ever saw, 'and the only one of his kind, he bowled what you would call a fast googly, he would pitch the ball well outside the leg stump and knock your off stump out, just like an ordinary left hand off break. I have never seen another bowler like him, either before or since I started playing, incidentally he never bowled to hit a man, but always to hit the wicket, if he could, and he very often did, his length was superb, which is everything in cricket, a master at his job.' The punctuation may be erratic, but there is no need to doubt the accuracy of this generous assessment.

By contrast, John was left-handed, never more than medium pace and often slower than that. But he was wonderfully accurate, could move the ball both ways off the seam and had one that he hurried through. His chief skill, though, lay in his slight, perfectly controlled variations of pace, so that no matter how well set a batsman might be, he would frequently find himself playing just that bit too early or late. In 1900, with Wass taking 108 wickets at an average of 18.82, the pair of them demolished several good batting sides. In the game against Middlesex at Lord's they reduced the home team's first innings to ruins, bowling them out for 119. Wass finished with five for 40 in 25 overs, Gunn four for 67 in 26 overs. One man, Beldam, was run out. They were largely responsible for bowling out Kent in the first innings at Blackheath for 98 (Wass four for 41, Gunn three for 35) and accounted for the Sussex first innings at Trent Bridge (Gunn seven for 37 in 19 overs, Wass three for 65 in 20 overs). Sussex were dismissed for 113, an humiliation that so stung the visitors that in their second innings they made 315 for 7 before declaring (Ranji 158). Even so, Gunn finished with four for 104 in 38 overs. In the return match against Kent at Trent Bridge Gunn and Wass took all the wickets in Kent's first innings (Wass six for 49 in 30 overs, Gunn four for 88 in 28 overs). Kent were all out for 150.

Not surprisingly, Notts improved dramatically on their position of the previous summer, and finished in fifth position. For this brightening of their fortunes they owed much to John Gunn. They also, yet again, owed a good deal to his uncle. William Gunn missed the first few games of the season, but had found his form by the time the West Indian touring team visited Trent Bridge in July. It was a high-scoring match and in Notts's innings James Iremonger made 101. He was overshadowed, however, by William Gunn who opened the batting with Shrewsbury, his old colleague, and scored a brilliant 161. He also took seven wickets with his lobs, four for 88 in twenty-two overs in the second innings and, remarkably, three for 12 in two overs in the first. The famed impetuosity of West Indian batsmen is clearly no new thing.

In the game that followed, against Kent at Trent Bridge, William batted with what a local commentator called 'faultless grace and skill' to score 137. Some idea of his dominance can be gained from the fact that while he and Dench were together they put on 102 runs, of which Dench's share was 17. Then against Gloucestershire he scored 73 out of 211 (the next highest score was 33) and 94 out of 227 (next highest score 38). 'The second innings of the home team was remarkable only for a grand contribution by Wm Gunn, whose batting in both innings was very fine.' The following week he scored 110 and 46 not out for MCC v Worcestershire. William Gunn played sixteen first-class games that summer for Notts and finished second in the county's batting averages.

The Nottingham Giant, though, was beginning to feel his age. In the summer of 1901 he and the county began well enough, with victories over MCC, Surrey and Essex, against whom Gunn scored 127. A little later, however, they suffered the appalling humiliation of being bowled out by Yorkshire on a tricky Trent Bridge wicket for just 13. William Gunn took time after that to recover his form. It had returned in full by the middle of July when he played what proved to be his last county game of the season. It was at Derby, and against the home county and Notts's close rivals Gunn made his highest-ever score – 273. As with all his major innings it was a flawless performance. Whether it exhausted him we do not know, but it seems at least probable, for he played no more that summer. Ashley-Cooper said that the reason was 'partly on account of a damaged finger, but chiefly owing to pressure of business,' but it is difficult to imagine that business pressures were any greater on him that summer than they had been previously, especially since Gunn & Moore had succeeded in more or less eclipsing their rivals. Perhaps Gunn's decision not to play again that season was strengthened by the arrival of another giant, James Iremonger. As was noted, the previous season

Iremonger had made a century against the West Indians, and in 1901 he scored hundreds in four consecutive matches. He became a regular opening batsman, and with an average of 42.61 finished second behind A. O. Jones, the captain, and just ahead of William Gunn (39.52).

That summer MCC gave William Gunn as a benefit the match at Lord's between Middlesex and Somerset. It was in return 'for his long and distinguished service with the club.' Of course he could not play in the game and he must have felt some stirrings of regret that his days on active service for MCC were drawing to a close.

For John Gunn the season of 1901 was a total triumph. Had there been Test cricket that summer he would surely have played for his country. For Notts he scored 1,149 runs at an average of 37.06 and took 88 wickets for 21.43 runs apiece. His highest score was 91 against Lancashire and on eight other occasions he scored over fifty. Consistency had now become the key-note of his batting. He was still scoring comparatively slowly, but game by game it became more difficult to get him out. And he was as dependable with the ball as with the bat. He took wickets in most innings in which he bowled and invariably performed with untiring economy.

He said in his memoir that sometimes he found having to bat and bowl so much in one game, and frequently in a day, 'very hard work'. But characteristically he adds 'still I stuck to it', a point he repeats in a letter to his New Zealand admirer, Robin McConnell. In that particular letter he is answering the young man's request for information about great players he had known. Among them was W. G. Grace. In the summer of 1901 Grace had written to Gunn, asking him to play for London County, which Grace was then energetically though not very successfully trying to run as a new, county-style team. There seems however to have been some misunderstanding between the two men, for in a letter dated 15 August Grace writes testily to Gunn, 'I thought you understood. I of course want you.' Then, perhaps trying to soften the tone, he adds, 'Congratulations on your bowling yesterday.' He was referring to Gunn's performance against Middlesex: 24 overs, 10 maidens, 87 runs, 8 wickets. In view of which it is perhaps not surprising that W.G. should have sent for him.

John Gunn did indeed play for W.G. (though not until 1904) but he remembers rather more clearly playing against him and 'several times got him out both innings in the Gentlemen v Players team at the Oval, he was a funny old man he often had two or three innings the Umpires were afraid to give him out – But he was a fine player.'

Gunn then goes on to offer the same praise to A. C. MacLaren. 'A very

W. G. Grace's letter inviting John Gunn to play for London County, August 1901.

❧ ●●

fine Skipper,' he calls him and 'a fine player'. He had reason to know, because late in the autumn of 1901 he received a telegram, which is now in the possession of Peter Townsend. It was sent from Kennington Oval, addressed to 'John Gunn Cricket Ground Trent Bridge Nottingham' and, in the tersest possible way, asked simply 'will you come Australia. MacLaren.'

In his memoir John Gunn said that being chosen to go on the tour of Australia meant that he had 'accomplished what I had set out to do since the start of my career, at rather an early age.' It is of course the dream of every young cricketer to play for his country. Yet Gunn's dream came true at an unfortunate moment, and almost certainly damaged his future prospects as a Test cricketer. For the party which Archie MacLaren captained was well below full strength and as a result had a hard winter of it.

Lord Hawke, the autocratic Yorkshire captain, upset plans most by denying MacLaren the services of George Hirst and Wilfred Rhodes. (He was also to refuse to release key players for the crucial Test match at Old Trafford in the following summer of 1902 – a match England lost by only three runs: not for nothing has it been said of Hawke that he lost more Tests for England than any other cricketer, although he never played in one.) The absence of Hirst and Rhodes was bad enough. What made matters worse was that several leading amateurs – among them Fry and Ranjitsinhji – declared themselves unavailable.

The party which left Tilbury Docks in the autumn of 1901 was therefore by no means the first-choice side. Yet among the group there were good cricketers aplenty. Quite apart from MacLaren himself there was Gunn, who had been in such irresistible form that summer, Jessop, Lilley, A. O. Jones, J. T. Tyldesley, Braund, Blythe and the surprise packet, S. F. Barnes. MacLaren had insisted on Barnes's inclusion.

◆ ● ➤

London County v Warwickshire, Crystal Palace, August 1904 – John Gunn's belated debut alongside W. G. Grace and London County's final match. Left to right, standing: umpire, E. H. D. Sewell, anon, anon, umpire; sitting, C. P. McGahey, anon, W. G. Grace, J. W. H. T. Douglas, C. Robson, W. L. Murdoch; front, J. Gunn, anon. Unidentified players: T. B. Nicholson, L. de Montezuma, A. B. Horsley and R. M. Bell.

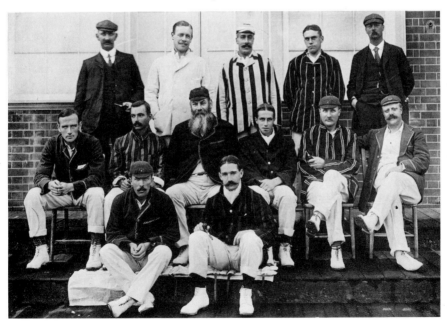

77

Nobody else knew anything about the man who had played his cricket almost exclusively in the Lancashire League. That was where his tour captain had come across him and formed the highest opinion of his worth. It was an opinion that the first two Tests were to justify. Unfortunately, Barnes broke down early on in the Third Test and from then on could do little. Which meant that John Gunn had to bowl an increasing amount as the tour went on.

However, Gunn could not have anticipated such things when the tour party left England. He would have been in good spirits: ahead of him stretched months of cricket and adventure, and he could rest easy about how his family would fare while he was away. His uncle had arranged for John's wife, Grace, to manage the Carrington Street premises of T. E. and A. Leake, tobacconists, newsagents and hairdressers, and it had been agreed that while John was in Australia she and the children would give up their rented accommodation in West Bridgford and move into the flat over the shop. On his return John was to take up an essential part in the managing of the premises. Financial and family matters thus agreeably taken care of, he was free to concentrate his mind on cricket.

He had a brotherly send-off. George, who for reasons we shall later discover was at that time working at nearby Virginia Water, met him at St Pancras to wish him God's speed and good luck. Very probably there was more to this than simple fraternal affection. Throughout his life John had as little interest in punctuality as he had in money. He rarely wore a watch, and on the few occasions when he did so it was likely to tell the wrong time or to have stopped altogether. He was always the last Nottinghamshire player to arrive at the railway station for away games. With porters slamming doors, the guard blowing a final blast on his whistle, and team-mates leaning frantically out of carriage-windows wondering whether this was to be the occasion on which his luck would finally run out, John would come sauntering along the platform. 'What's all the hurry?' he would demand to know, calmly taking his place. It is likely that George was there in the autumn of 1901 to make quite sure John did not miss the boat-train.

Recalling that far-off tour in his memoir, John Gunn said that it had been a wonderful one to have been on. So it must have been. For a young man from a working-class background the voyage out must have been exciting enough. There were sights to be seen – the Mediterranean, the Suez Canal, Port Said; there were deck-games to play; there was the luxury of simply being aboard a liner. Like his uncle, John Gunn had

The 1901–02 tour party at Melbourne where the Second and Fifth Tests were
played. Left to right, standing: H. G. Garnett, L. C. Braund, S. F. Barnes, C. Blythe,
A. F. A. Lilley, J. T. Tyldesley; sitting, C. P. McGahey, C. Robson, A. O. Jones,
A. C. MacLaren, G. L. Jessop, T. W. Hayward; front, J. Gunn, W. G. Quaife.

◆ ● ◆

started life in the humblest of circumstances. The majority of boys with
whom he had been at school were by now at work in the mines or in the
lace trade. And here *he* was, on his way to the other side of the world,
soon to enjoy lavish hospitality, to be treated as a celebrity, to play cricket
against such legendaries as Trumper, Gregory, Hill and Trumble, and to
sit down to dinners where a typical menu might well run to six or seven
courses and include exotic shell-fish, fruit and other delicacies, besides
having a full and expensive wine-list. That the menus were in French
would be unlikely to have bothered him. Let the meat be called *Mignon
de Boeuf à la Bordelais* or *Selle d'Agneau Rôti*: to a good trencherman
like John it would all slip down the same way!

Add to that the sights of Australia itself and adventures such as the
following – which John recorded in his own inimitable style.

> We had some really good times between the Test Matches out there in
> Australia, when we went out sight-seeing, and shooting, although I used
> to enjoy stonethrowing more than shooting, I killed a Wallaby with a
> stone, that was somewhere near the Jeuolian Caves, it was a rock
> Wallaby, and to kill one, you must hit it at the side of the ear, Mr A. O.

John Gunn bowling and batting. The photographs, taken by George Beldam, were intended for C. B. Fry's The Art of Bowling *and* The Art of Batting *but were never used.*

Jone's fetched me to have a go at this one, and I knocked him clean off a rock first shot, then took him down to the hotel, I was thinking of having him stuffed to bring home as a souvenir, but the Propietor of the hotel soon told me it was not in condition, all it's fur was coming off, so had to forget it.

Another time when we were out shooting, a fellow named George Newton and myself were lost in the bush, we left our party and went off on our own, but to my great surprise on our return, our fellow's had vanished, so we tramped up and down these great mountain's looking for them but with no luck, I had fairly had enough by this time, George Newton by the way was an Australian, and used to look after our team, as trainer, he seemed afraid but myself not knowing the danger's of the bush as he did, he made me laugh at his fear's, at last I came across something that put me in mind of goal post's and a cross bar to which horse's were tied, I made a dash for this spot, which I realised was where they had brought lunch up to us earlier in the day, George Newton did not agree with me at all until to our astonishment, we found half a melon, some-one had left at lunch time, we both were very dry indeed after our tramp, but soon sliced it up and quenched our thirst, that melon was worth a lot to us in that heat. When we eventually arrived back at our hotel, this was the next morning, my skipper [Mr Mac-Laren] wanted to know where I had been incidentally, we had to ride back on horse-back via an old farm house to a local railway station, where we re-joined the rest of the team, who had gone overnight to Melbourne, then on our arrival we had a game of Billiard's and waited for the rest of the team to come down for breakfast, a reporter who travelled with the team was standing by apparently to send the news to England, had we not turned up. All this of course happened before a Test Match [the fourth, at Melbourne] and we usually had three day's rest before a Test.

One other adventure deserves a brief mention. This is how it was reported in the *Nottingham Guardian*.

Arriving at Perth towards the end of the tour the Englishmen found themselves billed to participate in an 'International Football Match' and with fear and trembling they turned out on a perfect enclosure. At an inclusive charge of 6d, £89 was taken at the gates and England triumphed by four goals to nil. John Gunn, whose skill has been demonstrated to many a Nottingham Assemblage, played outside left and had the distinction of scoring two of the goals.

Presumably his games with Forest's reserves served him well in the match at Perth. But although his appearance on the wing might have evoked some memories of his uncle, we do not suggest that this 'International Football Match' justifies his being called a double international.

On the cricket field he really was playing for his country, but matters did not go the Englishmen's way. True, they won the First Test easily enough, by an innings and 124 runs. Out of a total of 464, MacLaren scored a fine 116 and Lilley a valuable 84. Gunn batted at number nine and scored a useful 21, but he did very little bowling. This was perhaps understandable, as between them Barnes, Braund and Blythe took care of the Australian batting. In the first innings Gunn was called on for only five overs and in the second innings he did not bowl at all. It is less understandable, however, that he should have bowled so little in the Second Test, which Australia won by 229 runs. Barnes once again bowled magnificently. He finished with six for 42 in Australia's first innings of 112. In their second innings, when they scored 353, his figures were seven for 121 in 64 overs. In that innings John Gunn was given a mere six overs, while Braund and Blythe, on the other hand, bowled a total of 84 overs, had 199 runs hit off them, and took two wickets. England's innings of 61 and 175 were sorry affairs, and Gunn, having moved up to number six, did poorly (0 and 2).

His opportunity came in the Third Test. Australia won an excellent match by four wickets. Out of England's first innings of 388 Gunn, who had dropped back down to number nine, scored 24. Barnes was injured

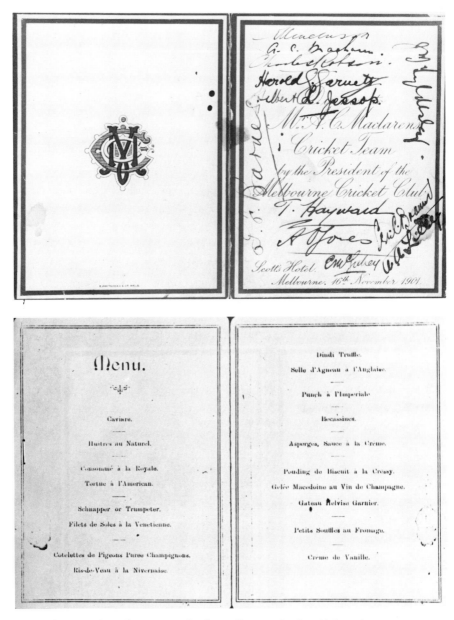

The menu for a dinner given by the Melbourne Cricket Club to the 1901–02 tourists.

after bowling a mere seven overs in Australia's first innings and it was then, and it seems in some desperation, that MacLaren turned to Gunn. Australia were subsequently all out for 321 and in 42 overs the Notts allrounder took five for 76. Braund's three for 143 in 46 overs looks, by comparison, distinctly prodigal, and leads one to question why MacLaren did not vary his attack more. His biographer, Michael Down, argues that MacLaren was a shrewd captain. Perhaps he was. Yet his reluctance to use John Gunn until he positively had to does not suggest great flexibility or sense; nor does his reliance on Braund and Blythe who, no matter what their qualities, or potential, were plainly not in Gunn's class. That was shown clearly enough in Australia's second innings, where the match was clinched with a total of 315 for 6: Gunn took three for 88 in 22 overs, whereas Braund had 0 for 79 in 14 overs and Blythe, although less expensive, was equally ineffective and finished with 0 for 66 from 23 overs. Had Barnes been able to bowl England would surely have won – although in that case Gunn would probably have spent much more of his time in the covers.

But perhaps this is unfair. And certainly it was not only or particularly the captain's decisions which affected the outcome of the series. It is worth noting that in England's first innings at Adelaide no fewer than three of their key batsmen were adjudged to have been run out: Mac-Laren when he had made 67, Hayward when he had reached 90, and Jones when only five. In his memoir, John Gunn remarked that 'we had no luck in these matches, some how, things seemed to go wrong for us, I must say some of the decision's made by one umpire there made all the difference to us winning or not, in fact Mr MacLaren objected to him at the finish, and then old Charlie Bannerman umpired in the remaining matche's, he was a little better, but it was too late by then.' Bannerman came in for the Fourth and Fifth Tests and it would appear that the three run-out decisions in the Third Test were the cause of MacLaren's protest.

Yet, as Gunn says, by then it was too late. In the Fourth Test England lost by seven wickets (Gunn one for 48 in 16 overs and two for 17 in 8.3 overs), and Australia won the concluding Test by the narrow margin of 32 runs (Gunn four for 38 in 17 overs and two for 53 in 28 overs). Despite the narrow defeats in the Third and Fifth Tests, the tour has to be reckoned a disappointing one as far as results were concerned. And John Gunn's batting form was well below anything he could have hoped for. In nine Test innings he collected a mere 77 runs for an average of 11. But he   83 had good reason to feel content with his bowling. In the five Tests, he bowled 144 overs and, with 17 wickets at a cost of 21.17 runs each, finished second in the averages behind Barnes. By comparison, Blythe's 175 overs brought him 18 wickets at the cost of 26.11 each, while Braund bowled no fewer than 258 overs, took 21 wickets and conceded 738 runs (average 35.14).

All in all it is difficult to avoid the conclusion that Gunn was underused and that his captain has something to answer for in this respect. And yet we have seen that in writing to Mr McConnell Gunn insisted that MacLaren was a 'very fine skipper'. Perhaps there were match plans that went wrong; perhaps the injury to Barnes upset strategies; perhaps the umpiring decisions were more devastating in their total effect than we can possibly guess from looking at the score-cards – the fact remains that Gunn was given less bowling than Braund and Blythe, but that he bowled a great deal better.

Still, he did not complain. Typically an undemonstrative, phlegmatic cricketer, Gunn merely notes in his memoir that he found the strain of playing on such a long tour very considerable. It was partly a matter of the unexpected and prolonged heat. Then there was the amount of travelling that had to be done. And then again, the keen rivalry between the two sides meant that there were comparatively few occasions on which he could relax. Of course he rested on the voyage home. But after that 'you must start to play with your County again, so really you have played a lot of cricket, three seasons straight away, and you really begin to feel tired about half-way through the season after your return, especially if you are an all round player.'

Within a month of disembarkation John Gunn was once again playing for Notts.

Some months after his return from Australia, the *Nottingham Evening News* sent a reporter to interview Gunn about the tour and other matters. The interview took place in what the reporter referred to as 'the cosy little cigar divan' in the shop on Carrington Street. 'John Gunn has heaps of friends,' the *News* told its readers, 'and it is pleasing to know that he is well satisfied with the result of his little venture on the sea of commercialism.' The satisfaction did not last for long.

One problem was that during the summer, while her husband was playing cricket, Grace Gunn had to manage the shop virtually single-handed. With John's return the family had moved back to West Bridgford, so that now Grace had to walk to and from work every day, carrying or pushing her three small children with her. Herself physically tiny – she took size 1½ in shoes – it is hardly surprising that she should have found the going increasingly hard. More than one old friend of the family remembers tales of her having to rest on the trudge home. Not that the distance from the shop to their house was all that great. But at the end of a tiring day the two miles must have seemed endless, and there can be little doubt but that Grace lost heart over John's business venture.

For it did not pay. Unlike his uncle, John had no great business head, and among those heaps of friends to whom the *News* refers so warmly there were some who exploited his genial habits. In Eric Gunn's graphic phrase, 'they robbed his eyes out'. The consequence was not long in coming. John Gunn gave up managership of the shop.

After that there was a little light work. For a while John acted as representative for Alton's cigars, which were distributed through the area by the well known Nottingham tobacco firm of Josiah Brown. But it was not congenial. Or rather, it was only too congenial. According to Eric, 'It never amounted to very much. He was supposed to go about taking orders but he often didn't get past the first pub. Mind, he wasn't a big drinker, but it'd be "Hello, Jack, come and have a drink." In he'd go, start talking cricket and that was his work for the day.'

It is unlikely that John Gunn was greatly disappointed by his business failures. But his form during 1902 must have weighed on him. As the season wore on the rigours of the previous winter's tour began increasingly to tell. For Notts he finished with a batting average of only 21.31 and his haul of wickets fell to 68, at a cost of 23.47 each. He can hardly have been surprised that he wasn't called on to play for England in the great Test series of that summer. Nevertheless, when the Australians came to Trent Bridge John had a fine game for Notts, scoring 80 in the first innings and following that with a useful 30. And when the Australians batted he was far and away the best of the Notts bowlers, taking six for 63.

That autumn he gave up football. Eric Gunn says he did so because he feared an injury to his legs which might affect his future in cricket. He was therefore at first content to busy himself with domestic affairs, and with the Lady Bay male voice choir. It was a good choir, with a reputation to maintain. Each Thursday there would be practice sessions, at Christmas there were tours of the streets of West Bridgford, and at other times the choir would perform at concerts and less formal evenings. However, 85

John must have missed many of those events, for he spent a part of the winter playing cricket in Johannesburg.

Obviously the engagement was of financial advantage. But not all winters would bring these extra earnings. How could John Gunn afford so easy-going a life? The answer is that Notts paid him well enough for the family to be able to rub along perfectly happily. And the Gunns were a happy family. People recall either from their own memories or the stories of others just how good a family man John was: kindly, jolly and entertaining, not only with his own children but also with those of neighbours. For he and Grace were excellent neighbours: generous and warm-hearted to those in trouble, always willing to help. One such way was to take others' children to Trent Bridge whenever cricket was on. Grace regularly sat and watched while John was playing, and in addition to her own small children she frequently had with her those of bed-ridden or poorly neighbours. In the summer of 1903 there was much to watch.

It was of course a season overshadowed by one particular event: the death by suicide in May of Arthur Shrewsbury. Not surprisingly, the team took some time to recover from this sad affair. But eventually they did so and by the end of the season they had moved up to fifth in the county table. Much of the credit for that must go to John Gunn.

In 1903 he did the double for the first time. For the county he scored 1,517 runs at an average of 45.97 and his 108 wickets cost him a mere 18.47 each. Recalling the achievement in his memoirs he says that he 'attained one hundred wickets and one thousand runs, for four year's running that was in 1903–4–5–6, after that I began to find it was too much of a strain to keep it up for too long a period, the fact was we played so few matches in those days, you could not afford to miss an innings or you would not make the double.' Which is undoubtedly true. But it was also the case that by 1907 A. W. Hallam had developed so well as a bowler that he and Wass began to do the bulk of the bowling, leaving John Gunn free to concentrate on his batting.

That lay in the future. So far as 1903 was concerned John Gunn's performance as an allrounder was outstanding. Among his more sensational games were those against Surrey at the Oval, where he had match figures of 14 for 132, and the following game against Essex at Clacton, where his figures were 14 for 174. In both games he bowled unchanged throughout each innings. In another game, against Kent at Catford, his first nine overs were maidens.

And then there was his batting. In that first golden summer he scored

96 once, 95 twice, made 161 not out against Surrey, and against Middlesex scored a particularly impressive 109. But his finest innings came in the match against Leicestershire at Trent Bridge. When Notts closed their innings the score stood at 739 for 7, which remains the county's highest-ever total. Out of that massive figure, and in a matter of just under four and a half hours, John Gunn scored 294. In the words of the *Nottingham Evening News*:

> Continuing to display wonderful powers of hitting to the off coupled with the constant employment of brilliant strokes to the leg and on, he set himself the task of creating new records. There was a tremendous outburst of enthusiasm when he equalled J. A. Dixon's 268, the highest individual contribution for Trent Bridge – curiously enough Dixon was his partner when he accomplished the feat – but the majority of the spectators had apparently overlooked the fact that after another over he had left in arrear William Gunn's 273 against Derbyshire two years ago, the Notts record.

John Gunn's record did not stand for long. A little later in the same season Jones ran up 296 against Gloucestershire, also at Trent Bridge.

His performances that season made him into a hero, albeit a reluctant one. Eric Gunn recalls his father telling him, with a rueful smile, of an embarrassing moment when, one Sunday shortly after his great innings, he was returning across the fields from the Trent where he had been fishing with a bachelor friend. (Fishing was a favourite hobby of his.) Some girls who were walking towards them began pointing towards the two men, giggling, blushing and nudging each other. 'They're after you,' John remarked. 'No,' his friend said, 'it's *you* they want.' He was right. The boldest of the girls came up to the two men and asked John for his autograph. Soon all the others were gathered round.

It is a pity that there was no Test cricket in 1903, for John Gunn would surely have been chosen to play for his country. Or would he? When the MCC party went off to Australia that winter he was not among those invited. It is true that Rhodes and Hirst were now available and not surprisingly they both went. Gunn would not have minded that. Indeed he had by now become friendly with Wilfred Rhodes and their friendship was to last long after they had ceased to play together in representative cricket, or to confront each other as keen but mutually respectful opponents. 'Wilf and myself started together,' John Gunn wrote to his New Zealand correspondent in 1953, and the two great cricketers still   87

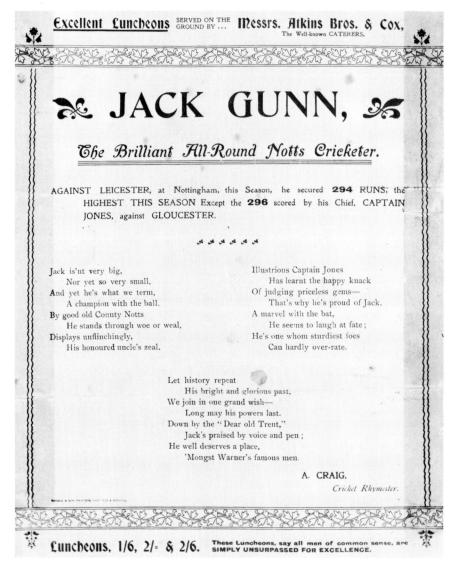

Frontispiece of a Trent Bridge luncheon menu at the time of John Gunn's 294 against Leicestershire in 1903.

regularly met. But 'sorry to see old Wilf now he's blind,' John notes, sadly. No, he would not have objected to Rhodes's selection. It looks, in fact, as though his own place probably went to A. E. Relf, who played for Sussex.

In the course of his historic 294 John Gunn had broken several records. One of them was for the county's highest third-wicket partnership. During it 369 runs were scored. What made the occasion so special was that John Gunn's partner was the Nottingham Giant himself. William Gunn scored 139 that day. He was now rapidly approaching the end of his cricketing career and he was doing so in style. The previous summer, when he had been granted a benefit match against Surrey, he had scored three centuries, two against Derbyshire and a superb one against Gloucestershire at Bristol. He finished with an average of 35.09 from a total of 807 runs.

In 1903 he did even better. Quite apart from his 139 against Leicestershire there was a flawless 112 against Surrey at Trent Bridge, as a result of which a grateful committee gave him £300 out of the match takings. (It made up for the fact that his benefit match of the previous season had, like the first, been spoilt by bad weather.) By the end of the season he had scored 1,011 runs at an average of 36.10. But he was now in his forty-fifth year, and it was becoming more and more difficult for him to reach and maintain match-fitness. Niggling injuries kept him out of several games. There were strains to his back, to his side, bruisings of thumb and finger. Moreover his sight was beginning to trouble him. And then, as he perfectly well knew, a fresh generation of Notts batsmen were waiting their chance. Perhaps Shrewsbury's death hastened his decision. At all events in 1904 he played in only four matches. The last of them, by the peculiar fittingness of things, was against Surrey, the county against whom he had made his debut nearly a quarter of a century before. After that game he stopped. A great career had come to its end.

Statistics, though, cannot tell the half of it. Herbert Strudwick thought Gunn 'the best forward player I have ever seen'. Another contemporary remarked of him that although 'some of his grandest achievements have been in representative matches . . . even more remarkable than these performances was the regularity with which he made thirties, forties, and fifties for Nottingham.' And having paid tribute to Gunn's exemplary patience, the precision of his forward play, the straightness of his defence and the fact that he is 'as safe a catch as we have in England', this same contemporary concludes that 'William Gunn is beyond all doubt one of the greatest professional batsmen England has seen.' The words are W. G. Grace's, and they come from his *Cricketing Reminiscences*. As a tribute to the career of William Gunn, cricketer, they cannot be improved on.

From 1904 William Gunn was to become essentially a business man, a model of rectitude in his professional affairs, stern but honest, and with the interest of his employees always in mind. Nor did he consider himself above them. He never lost his local accent and he regularly drank in his local pubs, especially the Lord Bentinck, with consequences that will be revealed in a later chapter. In retirement there would be much for him to look back on and savour. There would also be much for him to look forward to, even in cricket. For although he had ceased to play, the family name was still important in the game he had served so well. His elder nephew was already well advanced on a career that looked set to rival his own. Nor was that all. By the end of the 1903 season a third Gunn had begun to establish himself in the Notts side. Indeed all three Gunns had played in William's benefit match of 1902. But to see how that had come about we must once more retrace our steps.

6
THE COMING OF
GEORGE

In *My Cricketing Life* P. F. 'Plum' Warner recalls those many occasions on which the Sussex bowlers had been forced to labour against Arthur Shrewsbury and William Gunn. ' "Sta' back, Arthur," "Sta' back, Billy." How often had one heard that and how vividly are the figures and accents of those two famous batsmen painted in one's memory.' Yet by 1905 only memory could hold the door to the great past. Shrewsbury was dead, Gunn had gone into retirement. An epoch was over and done with.

But, a new one was beginning. Reviewing the 1905 season, *Wisden* remarked that 'William Gunn, after his many years of wonderful batting for the county, must feel keenly gratified to find his name borne with such credit by his two nephews.' That is no doubt true and we have seen how John had already established himself as an outstanding cricketer. But his younger brother's rise had been far less smooth, far less certain.

From the outset George Gunn was a frail lad, 'skinny' according to neighbours, frequently ailing. Thickset, physically tough, John soon adapted to the rigours of county cricket. Besides, he had prepared for it from those early years when he and George had played their interminable single-wicket games. The games had also served George, but not so well. He did more than his fair share of the bowling and fielding, and the undeveloped nature of his batting began to show when he graduated to local club cricket. In 1896 he was engaged by the Notts Castle side. He played most of his games for them in the Thursday XI, which suggests that he was at the time in trade or more probably helping his mother in the shop, at least until her death in 1897. None of his deeds for the club gave hint of unusual promise. True, he picked up a few wickets here and there, but his batting was very poor and he was usually last man in.

It therefore comes as something of a surprise to discover that in 1898 the county gave him a two-year trial on the groundstaff. No doubt his uncle's persuasive ways led to the engagement. But George was not considered worth a place in the colts matches of 1898 or 1899 and indeed he continued to play most of his cricket for Notts Castle. The two seasons were frankly disastrous. From 21 games he amassed a grand aggregate of 52 runs, with a highest score of 16 not out and an average of 7.43. The fact that he managed to take 15 wickets can hardly compensate for his wretched batting, particularly in view of the fact that when there was no county fixture John would turn out for Castle and always put his younger brother to shame. In one game against Forest Amateurs, a leading Notts club side, John took seven wickets, the other two to fall going 'c J. Gunn b G. Gunn'. In July 1898 John took nine for 23 against Rotherham and two weeks later finished with eight for 3 against Eastwood. George's achievements were by comparison trifling.

So it must have seemed to the Notts committee. At the end of the 1899 season George was, in John's words, 'sacked from ... Trent Bridge, because the coach at that time said he was no good, but I remember telling them they would want him back again ...'

Perhaps John also offered some words of comfort to George. Even so, George's future cannot have looked very bright. He had failed as a cricketer and he needed work. Fortunately, it was put in his way. On 1 February 1900 he became a nursing attendant at Holloway Sanatorium at the agreed salary of £100 per annum. William Gunn was almost certainly behind this. The sanatorium at Virginia Water, Surrey, boasted a particularly fine cricket club. In the old days, when he had worked for Richard Daft, William had seen how Daft's cricketing agency sent players, Notts or otherwise, all over the globe at the request of teams and clubs whose particular needs Daft agreed to meet. When Daft retired William took over part of the agency and no doubt recommended George to Holloway as a club professional, whose pay could be provided through his chores as an attendant.

It was a risk, for as a cricketer George had stubbornly refused to show skill or promise, but perhaps his uncle saw something that was hidden from other eyes. And there may have been another reason for his wanting to get George to Virginia Water. For among other things Holloway was a TB sanatorium and it seems clear that George suffered from incipient tuberculosis. (On a later occasion, as we shall see, he was to suffer from severe haemorrhaging of the lungs.) At Holloway he would be under the scrutiny of doctors skilled in recognizing and coping with the symptoms of TB. And so, early in 1900, George Gunn took the train south.

Virginia Water may not have cured the young man's TB but his experience of playing for the Sanatorium CC transformed him as a cricketer. In the summer of 1900 he scored over 2,000 runs and took a vast number of wickets. Also in the team was Humphreys, who would go on to an impressive career with Kent, and who in 1900 was outscoring George, and outbowling him, too. Perhaps their most spectacular success was in the game against Old Simpsonians, played on 1 September. Holloway declared at a score of 474 for 8, of which Humphreys made 207 and George Gunn, coming in at number four, 40 not out. They then bowled out the opposition for 44, Humphreys taking five wickets and Gunn four.

The following summer was even more extraordinary. Their best performance was against the Peripatetics, when they put on 348 for the second wicket: Humphreys 189, Gunn 140 not out. But there were many occasions to rival that one, and among them may be mentioned George's 116 not out against Surbiton, 123 not out against Hampton Wick and 115 against Colonel Fox's XI.

Perhaps the fast wickets, often chalk based, helped George's development as a batsman, perhaps he found confidence away from the pressures inevitably put on him in his native county, where his name counted for so much. Whatever the reason, the summers of 1900 and 1901 were all-important to his cricketing career. And it should not be thought that the cricket he then played was of poor quality. Many of the sides which turned out against Holloway contained county players; and the general level of club cricket was extremely high. So much so, indeed, that on 5 July 1901 the great doctor put together an XI to play Addlestone and George Gunn was invited to play. He took three wickets in Addlestone's innings of 184 but failed to score when he batted at number eight. Not very good, but then W.G. made only five and the fact that he had asked George to play meant that the young man's reputation was beginning to spread. Further evidence of that was not long in coming.

With the cricket season over, George resumed full-time duties as attendant at the sanatorium. He also found time to play football for Holloway. On 5 October 1901 he turned out at inside left against Kingston (Humphreys was on the right wing) and scored a goal in the team's 3-0 victory. According to the *Egham and Staines News*, 'Gunn with a stinging shot opened the score . . . (and) Gunn very cleverly taking the ball forward passed back to Greig, who added a third goal.'

Matters were thus resolving themselves in what must have seemed a highly satisfactory way, especially to so undemanding a man as we know

George Gunn to have been. His employment left him free to play all the sport he wanted; he was achieving some reputation as a cricketer, albeit at a relatively modest level; by the standards of the day he was not at all badly paid; and he had a roof over his head. Many a man has done worse for himself, and many men of George Gunn's day, and of his class, had to settle for a great deal less.

In fact his days at Virginia Water were coming to an end. One of the members of Surrey CCC, who had played against him and knew his worth, recommended George to the county and, since he was now qualified, he was asked whether he would accept terms to become a Surrey player. What was he to do? He consulted his uncle, his uncle consulted Notts, and before the 1902 season began George Gunn was once again registered as a Notts player. Which leaves one to speculate on what might have been. Or, as John Gunn drily put it in his memoir, 'They would have made any County a good first wicket pair, J. B. Hobbs and G. Gunn.'

George Gunn went back to Trent Bridge with a three-year contract. He also had a new companion, Joseph Hardstaff senior (not that he was called that then), who joined the groundstaff as a nineteen-year-old. And he was courting. On his return to Nottingham he had settled in digs in Springfield Street, West Bridgford, and was soon afterwards introduced to Florence Stapleton by a footballing colleague, Herbert Kirk, who was walking out with Florence's sister, Charlotte. The Stapleton sisters worked in a lace factory, their father in a dye works on the Vernon Road. (This explains how George and Florence would come to call their first son George Vernon; the second, equally obviously, was named John Stapleton.) Florence – or Flo as George was always to call her – was one of six sisters. She was slight of build, trim, and a good manager; theirs was to prove an extraordinarily happy marriage. That all lay in the future. First, George had to redeem his earlier dismal two-year spell on the Notts groundstaff.

His chance soon arrived. On 20 and 21 April he played for Notts Colts against the full Notts XI. It was a game ruined by rain and cold. For George, it was all but ruined by Wass. In the first innings Topsy bowled him for 1. Came the second innings and he made precisely the same score. It would be difficult to imagine a worse start. But he was given another chance. The annual colts match against Yorkshire was held at the beginning of May. John was now back from his Australian tour and came to watch. George opened the Notts innings. Three and a half hours later he was last but one out for 77, in a Notts total of 168. The *Daily Guardian* reported that 'Gunn's success was not surprising to those who had had an opportunity of witnessing his work in the nets and in the practice shed.' And the columnist added that George 'reached his fifty with a daring "draw" when he had been at the wicket for two hours and ten minutes.' In that reference to the 'draw' – a between-the-legs shot which had been favoured by early nineteenth century batsmen but which was by then antiquated and which is never played intentionally nowadays – we have the first evidence of that wonderfully unorthodox wit that

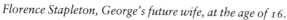

Florence Stapleton, George's future wife, at the age of 16.

was to become a hallmark of George Gunn's batting, and of his entire approach to cricket. What other batsman playing in such a make-or-break game – for that is what it amounted to – would have dared to play such a stroke at such a moment?

Two days later, George was back at the wicket, playing for Notts Club and Ground against Leicestershire Club and Ground. This time he scored 30, which if not spectacular was at the least a useful innings. There was no place for him though in the county side chosen to play the Australians on 8, 9, 10 May, nor was he included for the following match against Gloucestershire. He had to wait for his debut in county cricket until the next match, against Surrey. Typically, it came about in very unorthodox circumstances. He was not in the side originally chosen, although both William and John Gunn were, and both played. Notts won the toss and batted. By the end of a rain-affected first day they were 189 for 4. At that moment Topsy Wass went down with a severe attack of rheumatism and by special arrangement George took his place in the side. The following day he went in at number eight and according to the *Nottingham Guardian*, 'For nearly two hours he faced the might of the Surrey attack and if some opportunities for scoring runs were allowed to go un-accepted, he nevertheless exhibited an excellent defence and may be heartily congratulated.' Many years later he told Jack Robertson that when he had at first gone in he had tried to play some attacking shots. Arthur Shrewsbury, who was at the other end, came down to him at the end of the over. 'Stick to thy defence,' he told the novice, 'and leave the attacking shots to me.' Notts were eventually all out for 259 and George carried out his bat for 14. In Surrey's first innings he made what was described as a 'remarkable' catch at mid-on. Then the rains came and washed the game away. A third Gunn had set his mark, indelibly as it was to prove, on cricket.

As yet the mark was slight. In all George played seven games for Notts during 1902. He finished with a total of 65 runs, a highest score of 20 not out and an inflated average of 21.67. He usually batted low in the order, for the most part playing defensive cricket; but he made a good impression on those who watched him at the crease.

The following season he held a regular place in the Notts side and batted with some consistency but no brilliance. In fact his most outstanding achievement that season was off the field, when he married Florence. In the autumn of 1903 Flo and he went off to South Africa, where he had a contract to play for Wanderers – one assumes William's good offices

The Trent Bridge Battery comes together for the first time in 1902. Left to right, standing: B. Taylor, G. Gunn, T. G. Wass, J. Gunn, Coxon (scorer); sitting, J. Iremonger, W. B. Goodacre, A. O. Jones, A. Shrewsbury, W. Gunn; front, G. Anthony, A. W. Hallam, T. W. Oates.

◆ ● ◆

once more to have been at work – and there he scored over 1,000 runs for the club (including three centuries) and took 100 wickets. On his return he moved with Flo into 21 Byron Road, West Bridgford. Once again, poet and cricketer had established a kind of contact.

Perhaps it was a good omen. At all events, 1904 saw a rapid advance in George's play. He reserved the best until last. Towards the end of the season, in consecutive matches, he scored 86 against Surrey at the Oval, 106 at Leyton against Essex (his first century for the county) and then 143 against the South Africans at Trent Bridge. We do not have to look far to see why he was now maturing as a batsman. For one thing he was going in higher up the order – although he was by no means as yet a regular opening batsman. For another he had grafted onto his sound defensive play a greater variety of attacking strokes, especially the leg glance and late cut. In addition, he was beginning to show that love for fast bowling which was to haunt so many fast bowlers over the next thirty years.

The stay at Holloway must have had a great deal to do with this last point. It is doubtful whether there are any quicker wickets in the whole of England than there are in that part of the country. The bounce, however, is invariably regular and low. If you hestitate on them you are lost. If you are blessed with a quick eye and keen reflexes you can thrive. If, like George Gunn, you have that inestimable ingredient of genius which is given to few, you can both learn the necessary arts of batting and at the same time acquire the split-second adjustment that converts an orthodox stroke into the unpredictable, and against which no bowler, be he never so good, is safe. In later years, George Gunn would taunt the fastest of bowlers. Just how, remains to be seen. That he could do so is at least in part due to the seasons he spent at Virginia Water.

It would be wrong, however, to imply that George's transformation made him into an overnight sensation. John Gunn continued to take the major honours. In 1904 he made 1,086 runs for Notts at an average of 36.20 and, in Ashley-Cooper's words, 'if he had not been able to bowl a ball would still have been one of the most valued members of the team . . . He was very consistent for his only score of three figures was 100 against Surrey, and he passed fifty on seven other occasions.' And as it happened he could, of course, bowl. To prove it, that same season for the county he took 106 wickets at a cost each of 24.24. This included a hat-trick from his first three balls of the second innings against Derbyshire at Chesterfield.

The following summer was, as with so many summers in cricket's Golden Age, wet. It made little difference to John Gunn. He scored 1,203 runs for Notts at an average of 37.59. There were centuries against Kent, Leicestershire and Essex and a 99 against Surrey. He also took 99 wickets for the county at 26.18 each.

He experienced a bitter disappointment in 1905. The Australians were in England and the First Test match was held at Trent Bridge. Quite rightly John Gunn was chosen for the England team. 'Tell Gunn expected Nottingham Monday' was the telegram Lord Hawke sent him, which is now in Peter Townsend's possession. Unfortunately, Gunn had a poor game. In England's first innings he was bowled by Cotter for eight, and he was not needed when England batted again. Nor did he get the chance to bowl in Australia's second innings (in the first he had taken one for 27). Bosanquet's second-innings eight for 107 was the main factor in England's victory by 213 runs. Peter Townsend recalls that John Gunn

admitted to being nervous at playing in front of his own crowd on so

John Gunn batting during the 1905 Test against Australia at Trent Bridge, his only Test appearance in England. His partner at the wicket is 'Dick' Lilley; the bowler is Arthur Cotter.

◆◆◆

important an occasion. His nerves cost him his England place, and indeed he never played for his country again.

But for George the great days were beginning. That season for Notts he made 1,187 runs at an average of 32.97. His best scores were 126 against Kent and 110 against Middlesex, both at Trent Bridge. *Wisden* now noted the credit with which George, as well as John, bore the name Gunn.

And it is from this season, too, that one lovely story about George originates. Probably apocryphal, it nevertheless deserves re-telling. It came during his century against Kent. George had been regularly flicking the ball behind square on the leg side and to counter this Kent stationed five men in an arc between mid-wicket and fine leg. They then proceeded to bowl at George's leg stump. George's response was to walk away to leg and late cut. 'He can't do *that*,' one aggrieved bowler said. The next ball was well outside leg stump. Seconds later it sped past third man to the boundary. 'Oh yes he can,' George murmured.

7
THE BROTHERS TRIUMPHANT

When George Gunn first appeared at Johannesburg he did not make a particularly good impression. J. H. Sinclair said of him that 'He strikes one as playing in a very half-hearted manner. This won't do at all if he has any intention of sticking to county cricket.' Like so many, both before and after him, Sinclair was misled by George's deceptively casual ways at the crease. There would be numberless commentators on and off the field whose view of George was inevitably modified because of how that batsman of the half-hearted manner dictated matters to the best bowlers of his age. George loved to make the most difficult bowlers look easy, the worst ones unplayable. All the cricketers with whom we have spoken who ever played with George agree on a habit of his that is perfectly well summed up by Denzil Batchelor in his *Book of Cricket*:

> The long hop trembled and descended. Another split second and it would have brought immortal ignominy on its author's head by bouncing twice. But when it was three inches from the ground (and not less than eighteen off the leg stump) the batsman solemnly played it up the wicket, as if it contained half a dozen mortal traps, successfully foiled. The bowler, heartened by this escape, bowled his best ball of the season – of perfect length, pitching six inches wide of the off stump and fizzing back on to middle and leg. The batsman square cut it nonchalantly for four. You will not need to be told that the batsman was George Gunn.

The truth is that George's method was founded, like his uncle's, on a classic defensive technique. As a commentator wrote in the *Nottingham News*: 'Behind his audacities there were ingrained in him the stern principles that you must not chance your arm at the ball going away or pull against the break. Actions of this kind are simply unthinkable to a Gunn.'

John Gunn, the gregarious family man, with his wife Grace and their three children, Cyril (born 1898), Connie (1899) and John William (1896).

A studio photograph of George Vernon Gunn, George and Florence's first son, on his fourth birthday.

By the end of the 1905 season it had become obvious to all observers of the game that, no matter how apparently wayward George's manner, he was clearly a batsman out of the ordinary. His domestic life was, however, ordinary in the extreme. No flamboyance there, no scandal, rather a settled sort of happiness. That summer Florence had produced their first son, George Vernon. During the winter George joined John in singing with the Lady Bay male voice choir and now and then he played a little football. But by and large he and Florence, as so many of their neighbours recall, 'kept themselves to themselves'. Unlike John, the gregarious family man – he now had three children, and Eric would be born the following summer – George found his chief happiness at home with Florence, and he was at his most content when playing the piano. We have spoken to several people who think that George could easily have earned his living as a professional accompanist, so great was his talent, so delicate and sensitive his playing. But whatever George's private ambitions may have been his piano playing remained an amateur love, one that was to last him through his life.

It must have been at about this time that William Gunn began to think of his younger nephew as a possible junior partner in his firm. Gunn & Moore had by now developed an outstanding reputation for the quality of its products, and business was thriving and expanding. John's one venture into the business word had proved a minor disaster, but it was obvious that George was a different kettle of fish. At all events, it seems that his uncle wished him to enter the firm and it is probable that in the winter of 1905–06 George was learning something of the mysteries of business affairs. Then it was once more time for cricket.

At first all went well. Notts had a fine start to the championship season and both Gunns were to the forefront of things. And for John that was how matters stayed. Indeed, by the end of the season 'the great allround man of the team', as Ashley-Cooper calls him, had scored 1,312 runs at an average of 37.49, including 112 against the West Indians and 106 against Surrey, and taken 110 wickets at 20.72. It was during this season that, heavier than he had been when he started, he made the decision to switch to the slow, fuller-flighted bowling that from now on was to be his regular style. Bowling at a slower pace he was better able to exploit spin and variation of pace and, as the *Nottingham Guardian* observed, 'keeping a wonderful length he had the batsmen constantly in difficulties.' Probably his best performance was against Derbyshire, the county against whom two seasons before he had done the hat-trick. Now he took seven for 75 and four for 78. His seven for 86 against Yorkshire at Dewsbury was also an outstanding performance.

For John, then, it was a splendid season. But George, poor George. He went into July like a champion, scoring runs very much as he pleased. Then, quite suddenly, he had a most severe attack of haemorrhaging of the lungs. He played no more that season. The *Nottingham Guardian* for 30 July reported that 'the illness which has unhappily overtaken George Gunn . . . will incapacitate him for the rest of the season . . . he has done many fine things this season in spite of the fact that his health had not been completely satisfactory and his absence will be severely felt.'

As soon as the county could arrange matters it packed him off to New Zealand for the winter. He was put on board the SS *Corinth* and travelled out with an amateur MCC party, among whom was his Notts team-mate Mr G. T. Branston, so that he was not left entirely to his own devices. Still, it must have been a miserable time for both George and his young wife, separated and unsure as to the future. Tuberculosis, if that was the nature of George's illness, was still a fatal disease and even supposing he came through there was the worry that he would be unable to resume his career as a cricketer.

He came home blessedly improved. 1907 was a wet summer, so wet in fact that all over the country batting averages were unusually low. George topped the Notts averages with 949 runs at 32.72. From the very beginning of the season he did well, making 70 not out in the first championship match against Northants, which Notts, having scored 205, won by an innings. The *Nottingham Guardian* commented that George's success 'came with special satisfaction to his colleagues. His temperament and skill can ill be spared and it was particularly gratifying to see him playing so finely in his first serious test since his illness.' He followed that with 48 against Leicestershire, 'a beautiful and faultless innings' according to the same paper, and it is clear that his strokeplay, backed by an impeccable technique, was now so varied, precise and adroit that he charmed spectators wherever he played. Thus his 65 against Gloucestershire was described as 'the most polished and correct innings', while in the second innings of the return match against Northants George scored 84 and 'his stylish batting was always good to watch, and he raised the onlookers to enthusiasm by several beautiful cuts and off-drives, perfectly timed.' A master batsman was declaring himself.

John also did well, finishing second in the averages, with 30.92. He now began to bowl less, mainly because of the rapid advance of Hallam,

The Notts Championship-winning side of 1907, with the Gunns distinguished by their unusual headgear. Left to right, standing: F. Roberts (umpire), J. W. Day, E. B. Alletson, A. W. Hallam, B. Taylor, G. Gunn, umpire; sitting, J. Hardstaff, T. G. Wass, J. Gunn, T. Oates, W. Paynton, J. Iremonger.

and because in that wet summer Wass, with Hallam's aid, devastated team after team. In the summer of 1907 Wass took 163 wickets, Hallam 156. In the last championship match of the season Notts played Lancashire. The wicket was rain-affected, and MacLaren asked Wass what he thought of it. The great bowler studied the wicket carefully, scratched his head and made what was for him an unusually lengthy pronouncement. 'Lancsheer 'on't win this ma-ach.' He then took five for 42 in Lancashire's first innings and four for 18 in their second (Hallam took four for 36 and five for 16). Not surprisingly Notts finished first in the championship, an achievement marked by a heavily supported public subscription, organized by the local newspapers. The money was divided amongst the professionals and Wass and Hallam received £100 each, the Gunns £90. The triumphant team also acquired a cornet-playing supporter who, by the latter half of the season, had mastered 'See the conquering hero comes', which he would play whenever Notts took the field. In the Surrey match poor Tom Hayward had to march back to the pavilion to the strains of 'Goodbye Tommy'.

The Notts committee, though, were still seriously concerned about George's health. No doubt their concern was sharpened by the presence of William Gunn, for that great man was now a member of the management sub-committee, a singular mark of honour to an ex-professional cricketer. Any recurrence of the haemorrhaging of the previous summer would almost certainly put George out of the game and that would be bad not only for him but for the county, whose best batsman he was now becoming. Fortunately, a solution to their problems was close at hand. A. O. Jones, the county captain, had been invited to take the MCC party to Australia for the winter of 1907–08. Why should George not go with them? A few months in the dry heat of Australia would do him the world of good and in the unlikely event of the party needing a replacement he would be there. MCC offered him terms of £15 for each up-country match they would ask him to play in, and also offered him the job of scorer. He accepted. It would mean another lonely winter for Florence and the child, but it would help to seal George's recovery. That it would come to mean much more than that was not something either man or wife could have known when, in October 1907, they said their farewells. The best part of six months were to elapse before they would see each other again.

The tour started well enough. Against South Australia the batsmen ran up a massive 660 for 8, while Barnes and Fielder twice dismissed the powerful New South Wales side for low scores. But then things began to go wrong. Hobbs, of whom so much had been expected, lost form. And then, just before the First Test was due to start, Jones himself fell seriously ill. F. L. Fane took over as captain and Gunn was called upon. On the evening of 12 December 1907, the day before the First Test was due to start, it was announced that MCC's opening batsmen would be Fane and Young and that George Gunn, who until then had done no more than score for the team with a pencil, would bat number three. There was no place for Hobbs.

In their *History of Cricket* Altham and Swanton report that the decision 'was a bitter disappointment to the young Surrey batsman.' No doubt it was, yet it also needs to be said that he never bore George Gunn the slightest grudge. On the contrary, they became, and were to remain, closer as friends than even John Gunn and Wilf Rhodes. Like recognized like. Whenever in after years Surrey came to Trent Bridge, Jack Hobbs (and sometimes his wife) would stay with George and Florence; and the

*The MCC tour party to Australia, 1907–08. Left to right, standing: R. A. Young,
E. G. Hayes, A. Fielder, C. Blythe, J. Humphries, J. B. Hobbs; sitting, J. N.
Crawford, L. C. Braund, A. O. Jones (capt), F. L. Fane, K. L. Hutchings, W.
Rhodes; front, S. F. Barnes, J. Hardstaff, Col P. Trevor (manager), G. Gunn.*

favour was invariably returned whenever Notts were at the Oval. Old
people in West Bridgford remember turning out in order to see George
Gunn and Jack Hobbs stroll together to Trent Bridge, and Eric Gunn
recalls dropping in at Uncle George's to find Jack Hobbs sitting in a
favourite fire-side chair discussing cricket: 'If you want to be a county
cricketer,' he told the young man who by that time was hoping for just
such a career, 'you need absolute dedication'. And in his life-story
Hobbs, recalling the tour of 1907–08, wrote with exemplary firmness:
'Let me make it clear that no friction existed between Gunn and myself,
either then or at any other time. We were real friends throughout the tour
and have remained on the best of terms down to the present day.' Indeed
the day before the First Test he was one of those who helped George by
bowling all afternoon to him in the nets.

Yet if Hobbs, like the great sportsman he was, concealed his dismay,
another member of the party made plain his disgust at the preference of

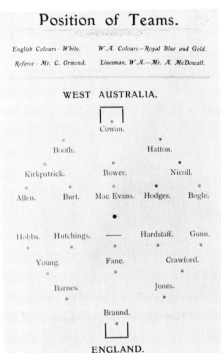

The programme for the football match between MCC and Western Australia played at Perth, 10 March 1908

George Gunn over the Surrey batsman. When George came down to breakfast that morning he was treated to some *sotto voce* remarks that must have rankled. However, there was little time to brood. The party was due at the ground.

At midday, having won the toss, Fane walked out with Young in front of a full Sydney ground, to begin the England innings. Eighteen minutes later he was walking back again, caught by Trumper off Cotter for 2. The huge crowd roared its delight at this early success. A moment's silence and then the slim figure of George Gunn appeared on the pavilion steps. The crowd settled down to watch its fast-bowling hero sweep away this batsman of whom little was known bar the fact that he was only playing by default. (Macartney recalls in his memoirs that when he saw the name Gunn go up on the scoreboard, he had to ask who this was.)

The crowd would have to wait, however, for Cotter's over had ended. Saunders now bowled to Young, who managed two and then a single, leaving George to face the last ball. It was short, outside the off stump. George hit it perfectly between cover and point for four. In Cotter's next over Young went, caught behind, and that brought in Hutchings. Two untried batsmen together and the Australian bowlers in full cry. No wonder the crowd was baying for blood.

What followed is of course famous in the annals of cricketing history. Hutchings struck bravely and George began to follow his example. But then, when it seemed that they had survived the worst, Hutchings was caught and bowled by Armstrong for 42: 91 for 3. Lunch came a few minutes later with Braund, the new batsman, not yet off the mark. George was 41 not out. Braund had still not scored when George, after a total of 78 minutes at the crease, came to his half-century. Forty minutes later, at a quarter past three, he stroked an off-drive to the boundary off Saunders and the scoreboard now read Gunn, G. 102. It was his sixth boundary off successive scoring strokes. At 3.43 p.m., after precisely two and a half hours, it was over. Hazlitt caught him in the slips off Cotter. He was fourth out at 208 and he had utterly changed England's fortunes. In his 119 he had hit no fewer than twenty boundaries and his stand with Braund had realized 117, of which George's share was 91. Shortly afterwards Braund was bowled by Cotter for 30. So slight and long-winded an innings may not seem to merit comment. It does however.

For the point is this: it was Braund who had made the disparaging remarks about George at breakfast that morning. Many years later George told Mr Frank Stokes, his neighbour, all about it. 'He'd as good as said I couldn't bat, you see. So when he came out to join me I thought, "Well, we'll have to see about that." I had strike and I kept taking singles at the end of each over. I reckon I kept him away from the bowling for about the first 45 minutes of his innings. After that, he didn't say much.'

Imagine! You are suddenly called up to play in your first Test match, you find yourself batting with someone who clearly thinks you aren't much good, and this someone is a seasoned international cricketer; and you simply show him what batting is all about, deny him the strike, go from 78 to 102 with six boundaries, and all the while you enjoy yourself. If that isn't genius, of a very rare kind, then what is?

Nothing, of course, could live up to that first wonderful innings. Yet George came close. When England batted for the second time he made 74, again the team's top score and he made the runs with his gloves full of

The Australian and MCC teams pose for the cameras prior to launching into the ample dinner at the Grand Hotel after the Melbourne Test of 1907–08.

blood, since his hands had become badly blistered in the first innings. Although he failed in the Second Test, in the remaining matches he made scores of 65, 43 and, most memorably, a chanceless 122 in four hours 47 minutes on a rain-affected Sydney wicket, where he needed no fewer than seven different bats. Jack Hobbs also batted finely in that game and in *Playing for England, My Test Cricket Story* he recalled how, after the day's play in which he and George finished not out on 65 and 50 respectively, 'George and I felt at peace with the world. We sat in the hotel lounge together, puffing our cigars luxuriously. Skipper Jones popped his head round the corner and greeted us: "Ah, yes, this is the time to enjoy a cigar, isn't it!"' George finished handsomely top of the Test averages, with 462 runs at 51.33. Hobbs was next, with 302 runs at 43.14. As Altham and Swanton justly remarked, the 1907–08 series proved that 'in patience and in beautiful method, Gunn has always been essentially of the Test Match class.' But the final word should go to Jack Hobbs. For in *Playing for England* he wrote: 'If any man justified his place in the side during that tour it was this great Nottinghamshire batsman.' Coming from such a source, that generous and touching tribute has about it the unerring rightness of true judgement.

In the years after George's return from his triumphant Australian tour the Gunn legend was born. Not, however, because he became a regular member of the England side. Quite the opposite. He became famous as the batsman who should have played on countless occasions for his country but who in fact played in only one Test match in England. That was in 1909 when George, patently out of form, was chosen for the Second Test at Lord's against Australia. He failed in both innings and played no more in that series. That would not perhaps have upset him. Years later he said that he had not wanted to play at Lord's, so poor was his form at that moment in 1909.

What of those many other occasions when he was passed over for lesser batsmen? Down the years it became almost taken for granted that the finest player of fast bowling, Hobbs excepted, would be overlooked for batsmen who could barely cope with pace at all. That was especially the case in 1921, as we shall see later. But the same holds true of the pre-war years. In his *Cricket Heritage*, written and published after the Second World War, Bill Edrich said that 'There have been cases where great players have suffered omission [from Test teams] because, in some way or other, they have dissatisfied one strong-minded Selector; Holmes,

George Gunn and, I have been told, Frank Woolley are cases about whom this has always been said.'

Yet the Gunn legend prospered. The scandal of his omission from the Test side was indeed part of it. 'Too much his own man,' some said, 'too ready to sacrifice his wicket.' And it is undoubtedly true that there were times when George would throw away the chance of a hundred. But he never did it when his side needed him. He did it only when the final result was not in doubt or when he knew that there was so much batting to come that he could afford to take things easy. Willis Walker has told us that on more than one occasion, as George and Whysall prepared to open a Notts innings, George said to him, 'Get your pads on Willis, I'll not be long.' Yet Willis Walker also insisted that George Gunn liked batting too well ever to throw his wicket away in a needless manner.

What is true is that the Gunn legend cannot be unravelled by studying the statistics of his batting, even though he made more runs for his county than any other Notts batsman. In 1908, the year after his Australian triumph, he scored 1,227 runs at an average of 32.29, the following season – his 'poor' season – 1,158 at 33.09, and in the very wet summer of 1910, a season notable for the first appearance of Carr and Whysall, he managed only 1,013 runs, average 28.14. Yet in those seasons he either headed or was second in the county's averages, for in such wet conditions batting was no easy business. But it was George's business always to make it look easy. And that is where the heart of the legend lies.

Everyone who saw George Gunn bat agrees on one thing: that no bowler could be certain what he would do. No wonder, therefore, that they feared him. How do you bowl or set a field to a man who is quite prepared to walk yards down the wicket to you, often talking to you as he does so, frequently meeting the ball with a dead bat, sometimes treating long hops or half-volleys with extraordinary, studied respect, then sending deliveries that would have been too good for most batsmen straight to the boundary ropes? Of the many wonderful innings that belong to those pre-war years two in particular have always been remembered as typifying the man. They came in 1913, a particularly rich season for him and one in which he scored six centuries and finished with an average of 49.88 from 1,596 runs for Notts. *Wisden*'s account is the most sober:

His two hundreds against Yorkshire presented the strangest contrast, the first one being slow to a degree (Notts were in a position of at best being able to draw) and the second amazingly brilliant (after being annoyed at the taunts of the opposition during his first innings).

In that first innings George was at the wicket for over six hours for his 132 and apparently the Yorkshire players offered derisory comments on his batting. 'Hast thou lost thee strokes, George.' 'Nay,' replied George, 'I haven't. I'll show thee in t' next innings.' And he did. When rain washed out play Notts were 129 for 3, of which George Gunn had scored 109 in 85 minutes. Such, at least, is the version offered by Gordon Ross in his *Cricket's Great Characters*, and there are of course variations on it – though not on the facts. George did make two centuries in the match, one did take him over six hours and the other did take 85 minutes (he came to his hundred after 72 minutes). And the wicket was, if anything, more difficult when Notts batted the second time.

That same season he scored 167 against Gloucestershire, which many who saw it rate as among the finest innings he ever played. Gilbert Jessop was one of them. In *A Cricketer's Log* he wrote of the tiring day he spent in the field at Trent Bridge, while Notts scored 530 for 9.

Long outings are apt to prove wearisome to the flesh, more especially to those whose bump of observation is underdeveloped, but on this occasion even an individual of this kidney could scarcely have failed to become livelily interested in the batsmanship of George Gunn. To see George Gunn at the crease is to realise the perfect control which a batsman can possess of the weapon in his hand. In some persons' grasp, the bat seems to wag the man and not the man the bat, and no matter how successfully a stroke may be achieved the aspect of clumsiness remains. With George Gunn it was almost as if the bat was merely a continuation of his arms, so facile is the execution of his strokes. I scarcely think that George Gunn was ever appreciated at proper value, otherwise more use would have been made of his services in representative matches. For this, I am inclined to assign as a reason the crass stupidity of paying too much attention to paper form and not enough to the actual merit of the individual. Nottingham cricketers have always been handicapped in this way by the paucity of their fixtures. Consequently in few seasons have any of their batsmen been to the crease as many as fifty times, which is not an unusual figure for many batsmen in other counties. As a consequence George Gunn's name does not figure in the list of those who have scored over 2,000 runs in a season, whilst many with less ability but more opportunities figure therein on more than one occasion.

And Jessop finishes his piece on George by remarking that, 'I have no hesitation in describing [the latter part of his innings] as one of the most brilliant exhibitions that I have ever witnessed.'

And yet, as *Wisden* remarks for that year, 'Strangely enough George Gunn was not picked for Players against the Gentlemen either at the Oval or Lord's.' Was it because, as Jessop suggests, his record on paper did not look good enough? Or was it, as Walter Hammond suggested, that,

> he got out dozens of times perhaps hundreds of times, because he was more concerned deliberately to irritate the bowler than to guard his wicket. I have seen him amuse himself for half an hour on end, apparently deliberately demonstrating batting tricks, careless of his score, and for his own edification – for he never cared a hang what onlookers or anyone else thought of him! He would snip out a single with the air that showed bowler and spectator alike that he could as easily have had a 4; and then crack a 4 away to the boundary off a dead straight, perfectly-pitched ball.

Is Hammond right? Was George so little interested in what others thought? If so, one can see why it cost him his England place. For such independence of mind would be unwelcome in a Player, even if it were to be found tolerable in a Gentleman. There can be no doubt that George did possess a demon of perversity and although Hammond saw him only in the post-war years everything suggests that as he was then so he had been earlier. Yet it should also be remembered that he could take note of criticism. On one occasion, at least, he had his own response to a spectator who had been barracking him for slow scoring. The match was against Derbyshire, the light was bad, wickets were falling at the other end, and George was doing his duty by staying in. (He was no doubt also enjoying himself by making survival look ridiculously easy.) However, his defensive skills did not make a favourable impression on a brawny miner, who repeatedly yelled at him to 'get on with it'. After about half an hour of this even George had had enough. He played out one more maiden over then sauntered off in the direction from which the voice had been coming. Offering his bat and gloves to his critic he said 'Wouldsta' like a chance?' Then he sauntered slowly back to the middle. No more was heard from this critic, but George, who told this story to Frank Stokes, had noticed the miner's size, and took good care to leave the ground promptly at the close of play. 'Just in case he was loitering. I didn't fancy a bout of fisticuffs with a chap like that.'

'Plum' Warner offers a different explanation of why George found himself in authority's black books. In *My Cricketing Life* he says – and he is recalling the 1913 season in particular:

> George Gunn was quite an original and cheeky batsman who played in an almost casual manner, but as to whose class there could not be two opinions. None too robust in health, he was a better player in Australia than in the often trying climatic variations of our English summer, and the Australian critics hold him in higher regard than many of our own, who view with disfavour his practice of getting right in front of his wicket to every sort of bowling.

This is interesting, if only because Warner was clearly in a position to know who those 'many' critics were. They were certainly not the many who went to see George Gunn bat. More likely they were the selectors of England's Test teams who, because of what must surely be condemned as a ridiculously unyielding orthodoxy, saw George as too unconventional to be allowed to play for his country. Yet the more one looks at it the more evasive Warner's piece becomes. If there could not be two opinions about George's class, why did he play so seldom for his country – unless of course opinion was unanimous about his being unfit to do so, and as we have seen that simply was not the case? As for the claim that he was a better player in Australia than in England – that is nonsense and must have appeared so to Warner himself. On the one hand he argues that Gunn was better in Australia because the climate suited him and on the other that Gunn was worse in England because he got right in front of his wicket. What has that to do with climate? And what was the result of his method? Simply that bowlers and spectators alike knew in him one of the greatest batsmen of his age. Besides, Warner himself goes on to say that 'anyone who has seen him at his best cannot but admit that there is something verging on genius about his play.' Warner thus joins Hobbs, Jessop and Hammond in agreeing that as a batsman George was *sui generis*. And, to adapt a famous remark of Shelley's, it seems to us better for George to be damned with the likes of Hobbs, Jessop and Hammond than to be blessed by selectors who were unable to appreciate his genius.

Warner was, of course, entitled to speak with some authority about George's batting because he had been captain of the MCC side that toured Australia in the winter of 1911–12; and George had been an outstandingly successful member of the party. Presumably he had been included because some declared themselves unavailable – Fry and Jessop both turned down invitations – and there seems to have been some discussion about whether he or Hardstaff should get the vote. In the event, A. O. Jones spoke up for George and he was therefore one of the 16 cricketers who on 29 September 1911 boarded the *RMS Orvieto* at Tilbury Docks.

Gunn's second Australian tour was not marked by the outstanding brilliance of the first one. But what he demonstrated, and in abundance, was remarkable consistency, especially in the all-important Test matches. Because of illness Warner was forced into idleness for much of the time and he therefore had the leisure to write an unusually detailed account of the tour. He noted that 'Once only, in the first innings of the First Test, did [Gunn] fail to reach double figures, and with a highest score of 75 he averaged 42.33 for nine innings, with an aggregate of 381 runs.'

It was, of course, a triumphant tour in which MCC took the Ashes by four matches to one; and they owed much of their success to the batting of Hobbs (average 82.75) and Rhodes (57.87). These two were the regular opening pair and George usually went in at number three. This is significant, as we shall see, because by the time he came to the crease the fast bowlers were likely to have been replaced by the spinners, among whom none was more important than the leg-spinner, Hordern. Hordern was easily the best of the Australian bowlers and he finished the series with 32 wickets at an average of 24.37. (In stark contrast, Cotter's 12 wickets averaged out at 45.67 each.) The English batsmen were uneasy against him. Indeed he was largely responsible for Australia's victory in the First Test, and Warner wrote at the time that 'Hordern's success during the last two seasons in every sort of cricket has been phenomenal . . . His length is well-nigh perfect, and, according to Rhodes and others, he also makes the ball appear to be farther up to the batsman than it really is. Here, then, are two attributes of a fine bowler, length and flight, and when added to these are the leg-break and the googlie, you have naturally a great bowler.'

In the First Test Hordern had established a psychological advantage over England's batsmen. Even those who could read his googly, Mead admitted, still felt uncomfortable facing him. If he was not tamed he might well win the series for Australia. The Second Test was therefore crucial. Australia batted first and made only 184. England replied with 265, but Hordern took four for 56 in 23 overs. When Australia batted again they got 299, which meant that England had to score 219 to win.

Rhodes was out when the score had reached 57 and George joined Jack Hobbs. George was out at 169, having scored 43, and England were safe. In the event they won by eight wickets and Hobbs at the end was not out 126.

What mattered was the nature of George's innings. When he came in Hordern was already bowling. It was to be expected. After all, he was Australia's main hope of causing an English collapse. What could not have been expected was the way George chose to play him. In Warner's words, he 'played an excellent and interesting innings. More than once he coolly walked down the pitch to play or hit Hordern; and though his style appears somewhat casual he watched the ball very keenly, and by a push rather than a forcible stroke made many nice off-drives, varied with an occasional single past mid-on.'

Hordern's figures for England's second innings were 17 overs, no maidens, 66 runs, no wickets. The spell was broken and it was George,

◆ ● ◆

The MCC touring party to Australia, 1911–12. Left to right, standing: S. P. Kinneir (out of the picture), E. J. Smith, F. E. Woolley, S. F. Barnes, J. Iremonger, R. C. Campbell (official), J. Vine, H. Strudwick; sitting, W. Rhodes, J. W. H. T. Douglas, P. F. Warner (capt), F. R. Foster, T. Pawley (manager), J. B. Hobbs, G. Gunn; front, J. W. Hearne, J. W. Hitch. C. P. Mead absent.

Menu cover for the celebration dinner given to the MCC team on their return from Australia in 1912.

above all, who had broken it. In *Twenty-Five Years Behind the Stumps* Herbert Strudwick, who was on the 1911–12 tour, remarked of the Third Test that 'Gunn amused the crowd by walking down the wicket to play Hordern; sometimes he would be 4 or 5 yards out of his ground and just pat the ball gently back to the bowler. This upset Hordern, no doubt, for he did not bowl half so well.' True enough: in the innings to which Strudwick is referring Hordern finished with two for 143 off 47 overs. The threat to England's chances had been finally dispelled. In the remaining Tests Hordern took wickets but they cost him dear, and George was – well, George. He scored 75 in England's one innings of the Fourth Test (it was in this match that Hobbs and Rhodes put on 323 for the first wicket) and according to Warner was 'rarely, if ever, in difficulties, his strokes being clean and clever.' And in the Fifth Test he scored 52 and 61. The match was played on a rain-affected wicket which so favoured Hordern that he took five wickets in each innings, including –

ironies of ironies – his tormentor's. But it was too little, too late, for England had already claimed the Ashes, and anyway, as Warner remarks, 'only Gunn could do anything with Hordern. Gunn hit six fours in his 61 and . . . his play was without a fault.' England won the match by 70 runs.

It is universally agreed that George Gunn was a great player of fast bowling. What is clear from the 1911–12 tour is that he was a great player of any bowling, even that style with which English batsmen traditionally find it most difficult to cope. And he used the same method against Hordern as he had against Cotter and would against Gregory and McDonald and the rest. He simply walked down the wicket to him, made his best balls look utterly ordinary, taunted him, played with him, outwitted him. And why? Because he was a genius.

As the tour progressed he also proved himself a fine specialist slip fielder and brought off 'some really fine catches', to quote Warner once again. How on earth could it come about that he was never again chosen to play in a Test match in England?

And what of John all this time? The keystone to his cricket was its massive consistency. When *Wisden* made him one of their Five Cricketers of the Year in 1904 they noted of him that, 'He is much the best all-round man who has played for Notts since Barnes and Flowers were in their prime.' Although, as we have seen, he began to do less bowling with the advent of Hallam, he can fairly be called a great allrounder. Indeed when in 1910 Hallam left the county game, John was, for a while at least, once again required to do much bowling and in 1911 took 49 wickets. However, he was clearly finding it less congenial than formerly and although he turned in some good figures – for example, six for 40 against Leicestershire in 1911 – one performance, against Sussex in 1912, during which he bowled 14 overs, took three wickets and was hit for 153 runs, must rank as among his worst ever. (It beats even that of our friend and colleague, Bob Moon, who once bowled twelve overs for 113 runs and one wicket.) John no doubt breathed a sigh of relief when Fred Barratt was recruited to the Notts side.

The spirit was willing, but for the flesh there were problems. Although his accuracy was largely as complete as ever, the tireless energy was beginning to ebb away and with the onset of middle years John Gunn began to grow portly. He also started to go bald and now always wore his county cap. Eric Gunn has told us that once, when he was chasing a ball to the boundary, the cap fell off and John bent to retrieve it, so allowing the batsmen an unnecessary four. 'He was a bit vain of his head, you see,' Eric said.

He was more rightly proud of his wonderfully accurate throwing arm. Although no longer the nimble-footed cover point who had run out so many batsmen in his salad days, he was still feared for his ability to send the ball, low and fast, over the top of the stumps from any corner of the field. Eric Gunn provides an amusing testimony to that accuracy. Once, when the Notts team was playing away, the dining-room of the hotel where they were staying boasted a cuckoo clock, from which the bird popped out not only on the hour but on every half-hour and quarter-hour as well. Its regular appearances began to irritate John. 'Next time it comes I'll hit it,' he said. Ten minutes later out popped the bird and was hit square on by a bread roll. Years later, Billy Flint, who was not playing in one particular county match, amused himself by standing in the crowd and shouting 'cuckoo' whenever the ball came to John and he had to throw it in. 'Dad was laughing so bad he could hardly see to throw straight,' Eric remarked.

If John Gunn's bowling and fielding were no longer oustanding his batting certainly was. Again and again in the pre-war years he was in the first three in the Notts batting averages and the only season in which his aggregate dropped significantly was 1908, when he missed seven matches through a compound dislocation of the thumb. As always, he was reliability itself. A typical run of scores – it comes from 1909 – reads: 77, 8, 47, 12, 23, 110 not out, 65, 40, 42 and 59.

He could also make big scores and, as the occasion demanded, would bat slowly or very fast. Of his 1911 season *Wisden* said that, 'Not for a long time had John Gunn batted so well. He could not get over his dislike of very fast bowling but he played many fine innings.' In the first match of the season he scored 55 against MCC at Lord's and it took him a mere 80 minutes. Yet when he and George had much to do with Notts reaching a total of 592 against Gloucestershire at Bristol he allowed George to outscore him. When George was out for 143 the two had put on 193 runs for the third wicket. According to the *Nottingham Guardian* John had a 'quiet start'. Still, these things are relative. The 193 was scored in two hours 20 minutes, and John's 160 took him four and a half hours. He finished the season with 1,368 runs at an average of 42.75.

Two years later he did even better. In the summer of 1913 he scored 1,397 runs for Notts at an average of 46.57 and, as Ashley-Cooper

The brothers triumphant. George and John go out to bat c 1913.

remarks, 'he was always to the fore on important occasions.' A glance at his scores will support that claim. He scored 92 and 55 in the victory over Kent, that season's champions, made a match-winning 52 not out against Surrey, followed that with 110 against Sussex and ran up 126 against Middlesex. On no fewer than 11 other occasions he made scores of 40 or more.

It is interesting to read newspaper reports of these and other matches in which he and George played sizeable innings. It is always George who attracts comment and indeed you have frequently to look at the actual scorecard in order to discover that John must also have batted well. The comparative lack of comment on his play is understandable. John was never as stylish as his brother, nor was he as outrageous. Any follower of cricket was naturally keen to see George bat, but Nottinghamshire supporters must have glowed with pleasure when John made his way to the wicket. For he was the old dependable: season after season he collected his runs, halted collapses, shored up an end, saved his county from embarrassing failure and put them on the way to victory.

Wisden commented on his 1913 season that, 'John Gunn was not talked about during the season to anything like the same extent as his brother, but in exactly the same number of innings he was within 200 of him in the aggregate of runs. In as much as he only made three 100s against George's six, he was really the more consistent scorer of the two.' It can hardly be counted against him that he scored his runs with a kind of phlegmatic, imperturbable calm while his more brilliant brother exasperated bowlers and thrilled spectators wherever he went.

In domestic circumstances matters were almost reversed. By the summer of 1912 George and Florence were settled in 46 Albert Road, West Bridgford, where they were to remain for the next 20 years. By now they had a second son, John Stapleton, and the family unit was close-knit and unobtrusive. There was of course music: but Eric Gunn recalls that 'Auntie Flo', immaculate housekeeper that she was, did not welcome noise and revelry. Within her doors all was order.

Or perhaps that was how it seemed to the young son of John Gunn. For at 9 Pierrepont Drive, where John, Grace and their four children all lived, there was a constant bustle of activity. When John was not playing cricket he was either helping Grace in the kitchen – making pastry was a favourite activity of his – or seated at the piano, boisterously accompanying himself as he sang popular songs of the day or practised the more demanding pieces for his beloved Lady Bay choir.

He was a great one for fresh air. The windows of his house were always wide open, and a nearby neighbour, then a small girl, can remember gale-like winds blowing through the rooms. She also remembers the stray dogs that used to follow John wherever he went and which frequently took up at least temporary residence with him and his family. George by contrast was a one-dog man. Mongrels succeeded each other in orderly fashion and all were given the same name: 'Chris'.

In the winter of 1913–14 John went off to South Africa, to act as coach to Durban. Perhaps he was now thinking of his future. He was approaching his fortieth year and could expect in a few seasons time to be looking about for an alternative means of earning his livelihood. He and his younger brother had established themselves as two of the famous names of cricket, but a name does not guarantee money.

If he did feel that his cricketing days were numbered he must have been all the more delighted that his oldest son, John William, was now on the Notts groundstaff, for this meant that a third generation of Gunns would in all probability play for the county; and even though it seems that his uncle had decided that John would not make a businessman he must have been proud at the way the family name was internationally known.

William Gunn, meanwhile, continued a much-respected citizen of Nottingham. As we have seen, earlier in the century he had been made a member of the county committee, and as Warner remarked at the time it was 'A sign of the respect held for William Gunn . . . that he was one of only three professionals of his day to have reached the heights of serving on a county committee.' He was also of course a director of Notts County and had played a major part in the negotiations that led to the old wooden stand at Trent Bridge being floated across the river in 1904 to form the main stand of Meadow Lane, where County now regularly played. His business continued to flourish, not merely financially but also in terms of its reputation. Gunn & Moore bats were widely acknowledged to be the best in the world. Each autumn Bill Sherwin would go down to Essex where he would examine his favourite stand of willows, mark some out for felling and then return to Nottingham where he would await their arrival by train at the Midland Station. From there they would be drawn by dray to the firm's timber yards, and highly-skilled craftsmen would set to work, under Sherwin's watchful eye, to turn them into the bats which were regularly bought by leading cricketers of the day and which they had made to exact specifications.

And so season succeeded season. When the Notts players reported for duty in April 1914 they must have assumed that all would be as usual. There would be a few new faces, some old ones would have vanished. But on the whole 1914 would be like 1913 or, for that matter, like 1904. They were not to know what lay ahead, not just for them but for the whole world.

8
BUSINESS AS USUAL

The 1914 season was a moderate one for Nottinghamshire. Early on it became evident that A. O. Jones would play no more; and by the end of the year, having suffered from a wasting disease, he was dead. Wass's great strengths were in decline and although Fred Barratt showed much promise there is no doubt that the bowling lacked depth and variety.

It is symptomatic of this fact that once again John Gunn was called on to do a considerable amount of bowling. As is to be expected, he responded wholeheartedly and finished the season with 37 wickets at 26.81 each. But his major achievement was with the bat. In all he scored 1,358 runs for the county and had the splendid average of 46.82. On 14 occasions he made scores of 40 or over, including 103 not out against Hampshire, 142 not out against Kent and 154 not out against Leicestershire. In short, the old dependable, now in his thirty-eighth year, was as dependable as ever.

George's season was not quite so good and certainly did not measure up to the spectacular achievements of 1913. For the county he scored 1,171 runs at an average of 33.46 and *Wisden* remarked with some asperity that although 'it would scarcely be fair to find fault with him since at his best he has few superiors, he is a batsman of moods and is content at times to let his hitting powers remain almost in abeyance. Why a batsman of his rare gifts should so often allow half-volleys to go unpunished is a puzzle we cannot attempt to solve.'

George loved to tease bowlers and spectators; and he was constitutionally addicted to the unpredictable. If he read those words of *Wisden* they would almost certainly have caused him to chuckle. But one fact is plain: in 1914 as in every other season during which George Gunn played cricket he was determined to go his own way, be his own man. During that particular season this involved a spectacular partnership with Frank

Woolley in the Gentlemen–Players match, in which the pair scored 134 in just under two hours, George's share being 54.

Then came the end of cricket's Golden Age. On 1 August Germany declared war on Russia, and two days later declared war on France. The following day the German army invaded Belgian territory and the British Government presented an ultimatum to the Kaiser calling upon him to withdraw his forces. As midnight approached great crowds gathered in Trafalgar Square. There was no reply to the ultimatum. The Foreign Office issued the declaration of war against Germany and it was greeted with round after round of cheers and the singing of patriotic songs. War fever was doing its deadly work.

Within the first few days of the declaration of war so many hundreds of thousands of men volunteered for active service that up and down the country recruiting offices had no option but to send them away. John William Gunn, John's eldest son, immediately volunteered and was taken into the army. But his father and uncle sat the winter out. Perhaps they assumed that the war would be a short, sharp encounter, the Germans would be taught a lesson and that, as so many prophesied, the men who marched away would be 'Home by Christmas'. If so, they were wrong.

By early 1915 the Western Front had settled into the weary stalemate of trench warfare which over the next four years was, inexcusably, to cost countless millions of dead, injured or hopelessly maimed. On 27 May 1915, George enlisted for the Army Service Corps. There was no question of his being conscripted since the British still ran a volunteer army. Conscription was introduced only in 1916 by which time Haig's murderous inefficiency and obstinacy had led to such terrible slaughter that the ready supply of men was becoming rapidly exhausted.

George did not, therefore, have to go to war. And yet the pressures on him to do so were no doubt as immense as they were on every able-bodied male. Quite apart from the White Feather Clubs, the chances of being hissed at if you walked the streets in civilian clothes and the endless poster campaigns ('What Did You Do In The War Daddy?', 'Your Country Needs You!', 'Women Of Britain Say, Go!'), there was the need to earn money. For nobody knew what would happen to cricket and the counties were certainly not going to pay professionals to sit at home when they could be serving their country. One reason for the vast numbers of men who invaded recruiting offices in the heady days of August 1914 was that the armed services offered regular pay, clothes and food, which came as a welcome alternative to those who were deficient in all three. Indeed the poor physical health of large numbers of the would-be recruits caused the authorities considerable concern and many were rejected.

In spite of his history of ill-health George presumably passed muster for he was not only admitted into the army, but from April 1916 to January 1917 served in France. He was then invalided out, according to Ministry of Defence records, because he ceased 'to fulfil Army physical requirements'. Quite why this should have been so is not clear. There is no evidence of his having been wounded. We must therefore conclude that he had a recurrence of those symptoms which 11 years previously had led to his New Zealand winter. At all events, once discharged from the army, he came home.

John, meanwhile, was serving with the Royal Garrison Artillery. When the war began he was already over the age for normal recruitment,

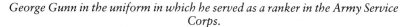

George Gunn in the uniform in which he served as a ranker in the Army Service Corps.

and even in 1916 there must have been doubts about conscripting a man of 40. Was he conscripted or did he volunteer? More likely the former. Certainly John hated the army. Once, when he had been home on leave and was due to return to barracks at Catterick, he simply burst into tears. It was not that he had a particularly difficult war. He was employed in the stores. Eric Gunn said of his father, 'I don't think he'd to work very hard. But it was the boredom you see. And he hated being away from home.'

Whatever the boredom, it was lifted by occasional games of cricket which increased in frequency as the war ground on. John played a few games for Pudsey St Lawrence, along with such fine county men as David Denton, Septimus Kinneir and J. N. Crawford. For although county and Test cricket had been utterly disrupted, much weekend cricket was played and indeed in the north league cricket was beginning to flourish. In his history of *League Cricket in England*, Roy Genders writes that:

> Many of the great county players who were unfit for military duties and many who were able to play some cricket on leave, flocked to this new league where clubs within a ten-mile radius of Bradford Town Hall were competing against each other like cat and dog. In fact, Bradford League cricket was considered to have taken over where cock-fighting left off! The clubs vied with each other in signing the most famous players in England . . . And Yorkshire's cricket fans revelled in this new style league cricket. Here for the first time were gathered together the country's greatest bowlers and batsmen doing combat against each other on a Saturday afternoon.

Not surprisingly, George gravitated northwards after his discharge. He was soon playing for Undercliffe in the Bradford League and therefore, as A. C. L. Bennett points out in *Weekend Cricketer*, would have come up against Sydney Barnes at Saltaire, Jack Hobbs at Idle and Frank Field and Sam Cadman at Tong Park.

During the summer of 1918 cricket began to return to more normal conditions. With the Americans having entered the war on the Allied side, and notwithstanding Russia's withdrawal, it would obviously be only a matter of time before peace came to a shattered world. Perhaps in anticipation of this, cricket's authorities began to arrange a number of representative matches. In July 1918 George played for an England XI against a Dominions XI at Lord's, was introduced to the King, and was run out for 36. According to *Wisden* he 'showed by far the best form but he took over two hours to score his 36.' He also played in the corresponding match at the Oval a month later and scored 24. He failed, however, when he played for the Bradford League XI against Captain P. F. Warner's XI, being out for 1 and 5.

That summer John played more cricket. Among the representative games in which he took part were Lieutenant-Colonel Hawdon's XI v Lord Hawke's Yorkshire XI, An England XI v Yorkshire (in the second innings he made 38) and Ripon Reserve Centre v Yorkshire, on which occasion he scored 32 and 39. He also made 48 for the Royal Artillery against Yorkshire.

Then came the Armistice. George was awarded the British War Medal and the Victory Medal. John was demobbed on 19 February 1919. The brothers had survived the war and they were understandably eager to resume their interrupted careers as professional cricketers. But for John's eldest son matters turned out differently. He, too, survived the war but when it was over he chose not to rejoin the groundstaff at Trent Bridge. Perhaps in the course of the war too much had happened to make him want to risk himself in a cricketing career. At all events he bowled his left-arm spin for Retford and he played outside left for various good local football clubs, but he did not turn to sport as a profession. The entry of a third generation of Gunns to county cricket was therefore deferred. Cyril, John's second son, had early acquired his father's corpulence (he would die young, at the age of 46) and although a keen amateur tennis player was not interested in cricket. Eric was only 12 when the war ended and as for George's two sons, George Vernon, now at the High School, was still only 14, and his younger brother was a mere seven years of age.

Thus in the spring of 1919 when Nottinghamshire cricketers once more reported for duty, the two Gunns active in the game were now approaching the veteran stage. John was in his forty-third year, George his fortieth. They no doubt hoped for a few more seasons playing the game that meant so much to them, but they can hardly be blamed if they felt that the war had robbed them of their ripest years.

The Great War inevitably made less of an impact on their famous uncle. Yet he had his own sadness to bear. On 28 December 1914 his wife died, leaving him alone with their daughter, Mary Florence. 'Flossie', as she was called, kept house for her father and entertained him and his guests with her piano playing, for like so many members of the family she was a highly talented musician. But on the whole it was a quiet, sedate life. William Gunn was not given to boisterous merrymaking. He was unfailingly courteous, he did not lack friends and acquaintances, but there was an unmistakable reserve about him.

As it happens we have a unique picture of what he was like at this time of his life. In 1916 Horace Murden, now an old man, but then a youth who had barely turned 14, was interviewed by William Gunn for a job in the Gunn & Moore shop. 'I was taken on as a lad. Seven-and-six a week were my wages. I'd to catch the seven o'clock train from Keyworth which got me to the Midland Station at 12 minutes past. Then I had to go up to Bill Sherwin's house – he was the works manager and like Mr "Billy" Gunn he lived on Hope Drive – collect the key to the works and go and light the boiler, ready for when the others arrived.'

'At the outbreak of the war they employed 24 men. That included Bill Sherwin's three brothers, Fred, Jack and young Mordecai. But by the time I joined they'd all gone off to war so there were ten old men and me.' The depleted work-force helped Horace Murden to develop his craft as a bat-maker. 'Even Bill Sherwin had to help out. He was like a father to me, showed me things I'd not have expected to be able to do before I'd served a much longer apprenticeship. But we had to get the bats made, you see. We were turning out a thousand a week.'

A *thousand*, even then? 'A thousand. They were being shipped off all over, and even in the war years you'd still get letters from the county men asking for their bats to be made according to their needs. Two guineas a county bat cost. Of course, it was worth it. Bill Sherwin used to select the willows very carefully, so's the grain 'd be about half an inch or five-eighths wide, lovely and straight. I'm not just saying it out of wrong pride,' he added, 'but we *did* make the best bats. There were none to touch them.' And of course so many outstanding cricketers agreed. 'The finest bats in Christendom' was Plum Warner's verdict.

Hard work and long hours, but Horace Murden did not complain. 'No, they were a very good firm to work for. I'd not have left them but for the second war. We had some good times. An annual dinner at the Town Arms, which Bill Sherwin always came to, and for which Billy Gunn used to help pay. But he didn't come to them. Nor to the cricket matches. We used to have them out in the Vale of Belvoir. Went by horse and cart. Of course, by the time we'd got to Charnwood Forest some of the lads would start drinking. It got so bad that on the homeward journey pubs wouldn't let us in. I don't think Billy Gunn would have approved of that!'

He remembered his employer's business habits very clearly. 'You could set your watch by him. He'd come into the shop at half-past nine

Gunn & Moore archive photographs of 1905 showing willows being sawn into rounds and then riven into clefts prior to transportation to the Carrington works for seasoning.

William and Mordecai Sherwin alongside choice rounds of willow at Theobalds Park, Waltham Cross, Herts (above) and Woodredon, Essex (below) in 1910. Mordecai, the seventeen-stone former Notts and England cricketer, was to die shortly after these photographs were taken.

Horace Murden 'joined Gunn & Moore in January 1916 when only about ten men were left, the remainder all being at the First World War. When I left in June 1940 there were around seventy people working, output over 5000 bats per month'. He describes here the bat manufacturing process as depicted in these photographs which were taken in the late 1920s or early 1930s.

Store Yard. Showing the rounds of willow trees being riven by beadle and axe into clefts as shown in foreground. Most of the willow used in cricket bats were grown in the Chelmsford area. These were selected on site in the autumn by Mr W. Sherwin, shown in front of picture. He was the first [Sherwin] member of Gunn & Moore. His father, Mordecai Sherwin, played for Notts CCC at the same time as William Gunn. W. Sherwin started by repairing county cricketers' bats in his father's outbuildings. The clefts as shown in yard are left for about nine months, then brought to heated sheds for final drying. This meant of course that one year's supply had to be in the drying-out stage before manufacture.

The blade making and handle making shop. *The blades are processed to the required shape and then put through a power press. On right of picture shows a small stack of blades packed in fours. This shows the blade after final drying out and then passed to the blade maker.*
The man seated is hammering the blade edges with a special shaped hammer. This operation is carried out after the power press operation to ensure that the completed bat will stand up to fast bowling. At the far end of this shop the bat handles are made as follows. Using Sarawak cane (approx ¾in diameter, 18in long) two sides are planed. Four canes are then glued together forming a 'slip'. The slips are then planed making a flat joint. Four slips are then glued together with three layers of rubber between. This then is the completed handle using sixteen canes in all. The shaping of the handle is then formed in a lathe.

Cricket bat finishing shop. *Showing the bat being shaped, balanced and weighed. A considerable amount of care and skill was important in this shop to get the bat down to the required weight and still maintain the balance. Mr W. Sherwin in foreground selecting a superior star autograph bat as used by county cricketers. Right of picture shows operators running twine on the handles and fitting rubber grips. Centre of picture you will notice midway down shop a hand operated press. This was used to bring back blade pressure after the finisher had trued up bat face.*

Two stages in the handle making-process referred to by Horace Murden. Above, Sarawak cane being cut into 18-in strips. Below, completed handles, using sixteen canes in all, prior to the final shaping which is carried out on a lathe.

The Gunn & Moore stock room about 1910, showing William Gunn at his desk and
William Sherwin; and in the late 1920s or early 1930s showing William Sherwin
seated in front of his order book.

every morning without fail, stop for about ten or 20 minutes, then he'd go to his office. He'd stay there till twelve-thirty. He used to lunch in a pub on Chapel Bar. If there was any urgent business I'd to go and fetch him. He'd always be up at the bar along with one or two of his cronies, a glass of whisky at his elbow. I don't think he was much of a drinking man but whisky was his tipple. And he always dressed the same. Dark suit, dark overcoat, and always wore a bowler. My, he looked tall. And he had a very brisk athlete's stride. I remember that whenever I fetched him from the pub I had to run to keep up with him.'

He also remembered William Gunn as a very good employer. 'Honest, straightforward, sincere. Mind, he was stern, but he was also very kindly. I used to go every Friday morning to order his fish from Burton's then I'd collect it in the evening and take it up to his house. He always gave me a shilling. When you were on seven-and-sixpence that made a big difference. At Christmas time the office floor would be covered with presents. Turkeys, bottles of whisky – I suppose they went to his business associates, but we always got something.'

Horace Murden also recalls that sometime in 1916 William Gunn began courting again. The object of his affections was a Florence Green, barmaid at the Bentinck Hotel, which stands on the corner of Station Road and Carrington Street, conveniently near to the then premises of Gunn & Moore. 'She was a very nice lady. Tall, very friendly, very smartly dressed. I used to run errands for her after they'd got married.' That was later in 1916, when Florence, as his second wife, joined William at 9 Hope Drive. The following year they became parents to a daughter who was christened Nora.

Then there was the matter of George.

'He used to work for the firm when he was out of the army. I can remember him always being about the place – for a while at least. Bill Sherwin showed him all the ropes, even how to turn bat-handles on the lathe.' Horace Murden's evidence on this point confirms that William intended George to enter the business. Certainly, when William Gunn came to write his will in 1919 he left three valuable tie-pins, a Nuggett, a Lord Byron and a Gold, 'to my nephew George Gunn'. But as we shall see, a split developed between uncle and nephew, with the result that in a codicil of 1920 William decided to leave the said pins to 'my nephew John Gunn'. Not that John was greatly pleased at the bequest. 'The mean old bugger,' he said, when he learned what his uncle had left him.

9
'THE YEARS, THE YEARS'

Summing up the 1921 season *Wisden* remarked on the fact that Nottinghamshire's team was 'decidedly middle-aged or more. The younger representatives are only Mr Carr himself, Richmond, Barratt and Staples. Oates, the veteran of the side, and still an excellent wicketkeeper, was born in 1875, John Gunn in 1876, George Gunn in 1879, Hardstaff in 1882 and Payton in 1882. Even Lee and Whysall were men of thirty-five last season. It is imperative that a team so mature should be refreshed with new blood.'

Wisden's concern is understandable. The Nottinghamshire team was undoubtedly at that point where kindly critics speak of maturity and mellowness, while the sharper-tongued mutter of decrepitude. Willis Walker remembers how difficult it was for young players to make their way in the side, for the 'old 'uns' were used to playing together and did not want to lose each others' company. When young Joe Hardstaff finally managed to gain a place in the first team he arrived early at Trent Bridge and crept nervously into the home side's changing-rooms. Fred Barratt was there before him. 'Where should I put my bag, Mr Barratt?' he asked. 'Over theer,' Fred Barratt growled, indicating a spot beside the door through which the young man had just come. 'Then thou'l't be soonest out o'bleddy door.'

Newcomers were not welcome – and, anyway, who were they to replace? Not the Gunns, that was for sure. Veterans they might be, but it made no difference to their abilities. That season George topped the batting averages yet again, scoring 1,647 runs at an average of 40.17. John was third with 1,178 runs at 33.67 and he also took 49 wickets at a cost of 26.88 each. The previous season, a comparatively poor one for George because illness forced him to miss several matches, he had nevertheless scored 1,008 runs at 36.00 for Notts while John had finished top of the county's batting averages, with 1,282 runs at 45.79.

'As a batsman at forty-four he was something of a marvel,' *Wisden* conceded. Precisely the same might have been said of him the previous summer when, in that first, gladdening post-war season, he finished second in the batting averages, on 43.65, and topped the bowling averages. In point of fact *Wisden* said that his batting was 'brilliant' and that his fielding at cover point 'suggested a man of twenty-five rather than one of forty-three'. True, his paunch was becoming more pronounced and his loss of hair was becoming so grave an embarrassment to him that in public he was now never seen without either his county cap or a trilby (he kept the latter on even in theatres and cinemas, to the impotent rage of those seated behind him): but his cricketing skills were as keen as ever and you could not possibly contemplate a Notts side without him.

As for George, he was clearly irreplaceable. Indeed, with the advent of Carr as captain George had become something of the team's senior professional. He stood at first slip, Carr at second, and George acted as Carr's principal adviser on the field. Off it, he was, as he had always been, his own man and it is arguable that the Notts committee was more in awe of him than he was of them. Flo always brought their dog with her when she came to watch George play, although dogs were not allowed at Trent Bridge. 'It's alright,' George once explained to a protesting committee man. 'He's a bar member.'

On another occasion, in a match against Kent at Catford in 1921, Notts needed to score 236 to win, and they were somewhat pressed for time. George as usual opened the innings and was proceeding with studied caution when his captain, realizing the need for quick runs, promoted himself to number four and came out to join him. 'Anything the matter, George?' he asked. 'Aye,' George said. 'I don't like the attitude of . . .' naming a committee man. 'He told me to knock the runs off sharpish so's he could get off home. I'll not take orders from him. You'll have to get the runs, skipper.'

Frank Stokes heard this story from George and said that what made the incident so memorable was George's delighted reminiscence of Carr's attempts to play 'Tich' Freeman, who by now was bowling. Poor Carr was out of his depth. He tried putting 'Tich' to the charge. There would be a great puff of dust and the ball would stutter a few yards down the wicket. Meanwhile George leant calmly on his bat at the non-striking end, occasionally offering a word of advice or encouragement. Finally he came down the wicket. 'You've got him worried, skipper,' he said. 'How's that?' the perspiring Carr asked. 'He can't work out what he's doing wrong,' George said. 'By rights he should have had you out half a dozen times. It looks like your day.' It was. Notts eventually won by eight wickets, with a few minutes to spare, and George's share of the total of 237 for 2 was 55 not out. In the first innings he had made 102 out of the Notts total of 264.

To this period also belongs a very famous story which has circulated in many versions. Our version owes most to Joe Hardstaff's way of telling it. Notts were playing Hampshire at Southampton. They won the toss and Carr decided to bat. At half-past one George was comfortably placed and, at the end of an over at which he had been at the non-striker's end and assuming it was now lunch, removed the bails and began to head for the pavilion. 'Not yet, George,' the umpire told him. 'We're taking lunch at two o'clock today. Back you go.' Without a word George turned on his heels and replaced the bails. He then took guard to face the next over. The bowler bowled, the ball was straight, George stepped aside and the ball hit his wicket. George tucked his bat under his arm and headed once more for the pavilion. 'I take my lunch at one-thirty,' he said. 'Good morning, gentlemen.'

He could, if he chose, bat with maddening slowness. In 1919 he scored 66 against Lancashire at Old Trafford, and of that 66 no fewer than 38 came in singles. But could you criticize a man who that season, even on paper, was far and away the best batsman in England, and who finished with a county average of 66.33. *Wisden* unhesitatingly called him 'the great batsman ... He was so consistent that he scarcely knew what failure meant. As in seasons before the war he had his varying moods, being sometimes very brilliant, sometimes unduly cautious, but whatever game he chose to play he was a master – always at his best with time to spare.'

1919 was indeed a golden summer for George Gunn. 'Certainly the finest batsman in England,' Ashley-Cooper remarks, who was going by what Jessop had contemptuously called 'paper form'. But the man's true genius came out in the manner and on the occasions of his run-getting. On 24, 25 and 26 July (a three-day match which came as a welcome relief, no doubt, from the two-day championship matches MCC were experimenting with that season) the Australian Imperial Forces came to Trent Bridge. They scored 371 and 242 for 5, and in reply Notts made

391 and 62 for 1. George Gunn's first-innings 131 was, as a reporter observed, 'so brilliant that his strokes drew applause even from the opposition'. And much of this against the bowling of J. M. Gregory which, the Notts CCC handbook recounts, 'he treated as contemptuously as though it were slow stuff pitched up for him to hit.'

Without doubt his greatest triumph of the season was against Surrey. The Whit-holiday contest always drew large crowds to Trent Bridge and 1919 was no exception. Over 10,000 people were on the ground on Whit-Monday when Notts, batting first, made 390 for 7 before declaring. George scored 169 and John Gunn 62. Surrey replied with 355, thereby making the game safe. When Notts batted again the object of the exercise was to provide the spectators with an exhibition of fine batting. They managed this to such effect that when the game came to an end Notts were 338 for 1. George carried his bat for 185 and John his for 111. Their unfinished partnership was worth 233 and on the way George became the first batsman to score more than 150 runs in each innings of a match. Willis Walker told us that as the Surrey fielders crossed between overs Jack Hobbs said to his friend, 'Not got enough yet then, George?' and George replied, 'I think I'll stay a while longer, Jack.'

Yet his largest score that season is not one that regularly features in the record books. A local amateur cricketer pestered George to play against him in a single-wicket match, the stake to be £100. No, George said, but after the man became tiresomely persistent he agreed, on condition that the prizemoney be dropped to £5. They agreed terms. The match was to be played on the Trent Bridge practice ground, it was to begin at five o'clock each evening and play would stop at half-past seven. George won the toss and elected to bat. News of the match had by now got about and there were several hundreds of curious spectators on the ground when George began his innings. Among them was a schoolboy, H. Silverberg, who was himself to become a club cricketer of some proficiency. He is included in a photograph of the teams who played at the opening of Sir Julien Cahn's Loughborough Road Cricket Ground on 4 June 1926. He told us: 'I remember that George was nearly bowled in the first over.' Perhaps George was teasing. At all events by seven-thirty that first evening his score stood at exactly 300. By seven-thirty the following evening it had advanced to 620. At that point the amateur suggested that George might like to declare. George declined. However, he offered his opponent the chance to bowl against the heavy roller, which was nearly six feet wide, rather than the three stumps. Shamefacedly the amateur accepted the offer and so on the third evening of this extraordinary contest George came out and solemnly took guard in front of the roller. An hour and a half later, when George's score had reached 777, the amateur finally broke. He threw the ball down and announced that he was no longer prepared to carry on bowling. According to some versions he then disappeared into the Trent Bridge Inn and only came out when he was so pitiably drunk that he could bear to face the taunts of those who had watched his attempt to humiliate George. According to others he immediately left the district and was never seen again. One thing is however certain. He did not pay George the £5 he owed him.

There could be no doubt in any reasonable person's mind that in the immediate post-war years George Gunn was at the very top of his profession. Certainly there was none in Walter Hammond's. In *Cricket's Secret History*, he wrote that George,

> was the only batsman I have ever seen who revelled in the fastest bowling. I could play it, and I have known others who could score off it, but none of them ever said they liked it. When Gregory and McDonald scythed their way through the crop of English wickets, some batsmen, among whom I frankly admit I was one, were afraid of them, to use a blunt word. Only George Gunn plainly enjoyed them, yet Gunn at the time was a veteran at that age when reactions are supposed to be slowing up.
>
> The first time Gregory saw Gunn batting, stepping down the pitch to meet the ball, he said to another Australian, 'He won't do that to me!' His companion, who had bowled against George said, 'Don't worry. He will!' When young Gregory first found Gunn facing him, he put that extra bit of devil into his tremendous bounding run, and sent down the ball like red lightning. After one or two balls, however, Gunn was running out to them, hitting them hard.

Not running. George did not run, because to have done so would have disturbed his perfect balance. Everyone – including Hammond himself on other occasions – agrees that George *walked* towards the bowler, advancing on him crabwise, head quite still, bat lifted high and straight behind him. It was a comparatively heavy bat for those days. The four-pounders of Lord Frederick Beauclerk's era had generally given way to bats that weighed on average two pounds two to three ounces. George, though, used a bat that was at least two pounds six ounces (according to Horace Murden) and possibly as much as three pounds (according to

Harold Gimblett, who was advised by George to use one of the same weight, and even given a couple by him to try out).

Whatever the weight of his bat, George used it on only two occasions against Gregory in the summer of 1921. The first was when the Australians came to Trent Bridge in June. Then at the end of their triumphant Test series the all-conquering Australians – their one defeat was at the hands of MacLaren's England XI at Eastbourne – played a series of friendly games. Among them was a two-day match against the West of Scotland. The Scottish side included both Gunns and Carr and the game was watched by the young Ian Peebles, who describes it thus in *Batter's Castle*:

> One of my fondest of all cricket memories is going with my father to Hamilton Crescent in Glasgow to see Mannes go in first, with George Gunn, against the Australians. They got 40 for the first wicket, quite an event against Jack Gregory. I can still see that magnificent bounding run and leap, with George advancing crabwise from the opposite end . . .

George won that particular duel, but he was stumped by Oldfield off the bowling of Mailey for 26.

He also won most of his duels against McDonald. In *Cricket With the Lid Off*, A. W. Carr recalls that 'I once saw McDonald, then playing for Lancashire, have a go at him with the new ball and with six men plastered on the leg side. I have seldom seen any batsman make any bowler look such a damned fool.' It may be this occasion that Frank Stokes was referring to when he remembers that McDonald came near to tearing his hair over George's ability to leg-glance between the cordon of leg fielders, but that whenever he changed his line towards off stump he would be driven through the covers or cut backward of square. But then there were many occasions on which George teased and taunted the fastest of bowlers. Although in *The Larwood Story* Harold Larwood has George say of fast bowling 'Nobody likes it, but some play it better than others', that somehow does not ring true. George *did* like fast bowling.

This leads to serious comment, prompted by Hammond's reflections. In the 1921 Test series Australia won the first three Tests and, no doubt relaxing because they had secured the Ashes, allowed the last two to be drawn. McDonald took 27 English wickets, Gregory 19, and England tried no fewer than 30 players. (Hobbs was injured for the first two Tests, chosen for the third, developed appendicitis and did not play again that season.) Nearly three whole Test teams, and yet George Gunn was never selected! It cannot be because he had a poor season. Going by 'paper form' George finished with a better average than Tennyson, Brown, Douglas, Jupp and Holmes, all of whom played in the Test series. But the plain fact is that the English batsmen chosen to cope with McDonald and Gregory were time after time ruthlessly cut down while one of the greatest of all players of fast bowling was studiously ignored. 'He won't do that to me!' But he did, and he would very probably have done it in the Test matches had he been given the chance.

On the field the England selectors overlooked their best chance to thwart the Australians. Off it, there was a time of real sadness for the Gunn family. On 29 January 1921 William Gunn died. The cause of death was cancer of the colon. He had become ill the previous autumn and according to Eric Gunn had taken a house in Skegness, hoping the sea air would do him good. When it became clear that he was near death, he was brought back to 9 Hope Drive, and it was there that he died.

William Gunn's grave in the Rock Cemetery, Nottingham.

His funeral was an occasion of some pomp. The boy who some 60 years previously had begun in such desperately poor surroundings was seen out of life by many to whom he had become a legend. William Gunn was an honourable, plain-dealing businessman who had succeeded to the extent that his personal fortune included his house in The Park, another at West Bridgford (which he left to his sister, Sarah Ann Bissill) and £60,000, the bulk of which he left to his second wife and in trust to his infant daughter. His co-directors, John Eite, Joseph Stirland and William Sherwin were left £1,000 each, Reginald Bloor £500, Flossie had the grand piano and, as we have seen, the tie-pins went to John Gunn. But to the majority of the mourners who followed the hearse to Rock Cemetery William Gunn was simply the Nottingham Giant, the great cricketer and footballer, whose sporting prowess had earned him international fame.

In a fine obituary, *Wisden* summed him up by saying, 'Few batsmen of his own or any other day were so well worth looking at as William Gunn.' And, after commenting on his natural grace of movement, it continues:

> Wherever he played he was the most striking figure on the field. As a batsman he represented the orthodox – one might even say the classic – school at its best. With his perfectly straight bat and beautifully finished style, he was a model to be copied . . . His 228 for the Players at Lord's in 1890 is the highest score ever made against the Australians in this country. The Australians as a team were not strong in 1890, but they had Charles Turner and Ferris to bowl for them . . . Asked in an interview whether he had ever felt tired of cricket, Sydney Gregory said he thought not, except, perhaps, when he heard Billy Gunn say 'No' at Lord's for seven hours and a half . . .
>
> Though he made bigger scores without number, Gunn never played finer cricket than in the memorable match between Nottinghamshire and Surrey at the Oval in 1892. His 58 against the superb bowling of George Lohmann and Lockwood on a far from easy wicket was a veritable masterpiece of batting. For an hour and a quarter on the second afternoon he and William Barnes withstood a tremendous onslaught. It was cricket that no one who saw it could ever forget.

So the years began to exact their toll. In 1922 Notts finished second in the championship. Cause for rejoicing one might have thought, and yet *Wisden*'s report was, if anything, even more fretful than that of the previous summer. 'Successors to the brothers Gunn, Hardstaff, Payton and the veteran Oates, will have to be found before many seasons have passed,' it said. And to be fair, the warning was necessary.

By the end of the 1925 season Hardstaff, frail echo of his earlier self, had gone in favour of Willis Walker, Oates had been replaced by Lilley, and a raw young man named Harold Larwood had taken 73 wickets in his first, less than full, season. On the other hand there was no getting rid of Payton – 'the best number five who never played for England' as the locals called him; and, as for George Gunn, *Wisden* was compelled to admit in the summer of 1925 'he still retains his exceptional skill'. He was by then in his forty-seventh year and he was no longer top of the batting averages, but to leave him out of the Notts side was unthinkable.

In 1922 George finished the season with an average of 33.95 from 1,392 runs, which included 109 against Essex – 'a stylish performance' the *Nottingham Evening Post* called it, and 180 not out against Hampshire, during which, according to the same newspaper, 'he batted with all his well-known finish'. The following season, when Notts again came second, Payton headed the averages and George, with 37.05 from 1,408 runs, was fourth behind his brother and Whysall. *Wisden* remarked that 'The Notts batting was . . . a model of consistency. Payton, John Gunn, Whysall, George Gunn and A. W. Carr were very much one in quality.'

Perhaps George's finest achievement that season was his 220 against Derbyshire, made in little over four and a half hours, and, as it turned out, the highest score of his career. He also made 118 against Glamorgan when 'he was on top of his form. At the wicket three hours, he hit 14 fours and gave no chance.' Against Lancashire he made 115 ('George Gunn showed his best form for three hours, twenty minutes') and there was an innings of 76 against Derbyshire, which *Wisden* notes was 'quite the best feature of the game . . . he scored 76 out of 120, his being the fourth wicket to fall.' No, he was not ready to go into retirement, not yet.

Nor was he in 1924. It was a wretchedly rainy and cold summer and Notts fell back to seventh position in the championship table. Yet as *Wisden* had to admit, 'George Gunn, allowing for the soft wickets, was every bit as good as in 1923, bearing his forty-five years very lightly.' On the face of it his championship average of 30.91 from 1,329 runs may not look anything special, but closer inspection reveals he was very consistent. He made only one century that summer, 112 against Essex. But he enjoyed some fine form, such as the following, unbroken, sequence of scores, beginning with a match against Kent where he made 98. He followed that with 82 against Worcestershire (he and Whysall put on 200 for the first wicket), 50 and 11 against Lancashire, 32 and 13 against Essex, 43 and 27 in the return match with Lancashire, 55 and 38 against

Middlesex, 28 against Yorkshire, and 95 and 1 not out against Leicestershire.

The next year, 1925, Notts were one of the best county sides in the land. They won 15 of their matches and lost only three. However, they failed to take first-innings points in the majority of their drawn games and because of that had to be content with fourth position in the championship table. George came third in the batting averages, behind Carr and Payton, with 38.37 from 1,458 runs. Consistency was again the hallmark of his play. He began the season with the following run of scores: 35 against Hampshire, 39 against Sussex, 78 and 67 not out against Derbyshire, 45 against Leicestershire, 117 and 20 against Surrey (the century took him four and a quarter hours, it was made on a difficult wicket and he did not give a chance), 67 in the return match against Leicestershire, and 34 against Cambridge University. He missed the next two matches through injury, and returned for the game against Lancashire, scoring 68 and 16. He followed that with 69 and 68 against Glamorgan, then made 75 and 28 against Kent, 7 and 78 against Sussex, failed against Hampshire, came back to make 49 against Yorkshire in his benefit match, and rounded the season off with 45 against Northants and 25 and 51 not out in the return game against Glamorgan.

He also played for An England XI against Lancashire at Blackpool early in September. In his one innings he scored exactly 100 and *Wisden* noted that, 'In a match of few batting successes, that of George Gunn stood out prominently. Scoring 76 out of 130 on Saturday, the Notts professional reached three figures for the second time during the season, playing masterly cricket throughout a stay of nearly three hours. Well-timed drives and leg glances produced sixteen fours.'

By the time he played that innings George Gunn had turned 46. It is not to be wondered at that he should be scoring fewer hundreds per season than in his earlier days. What does deserve our attention is the fact that during the 1925 season he scored 35 or better on no fewer than eighteen occasions, and that among those scores were twelve greater than fifty. Small wonder that by now *Wisden* had given up suggesting the need to replace him. Replace George Gunn? How could you?

Yet for the first time in many years there were occasions that summer when no Gunn played for Nottinghamshire. A younger generation of Gunns had not yet emerged. John William had given up cricket for the life of hotelier and musician. George Vernon Gunn, George's elder boy, showed great promise but was as yet a mere colt; and Eric, John's youngest, having tried and failed to get onto the Notts groundstaff, was forbidden by his father from pursuing his fortunes with Warwickshire, who had taken an interest in him. 'You play for Nottinghamshire or nobody,' John said. Eric therefore looked for another career. It meant that as far as county cricket was concerned the Gunn name was carried by the two brothers. But on a few occasions in 1925 George was absent injured. In the June match against Worcestershire he hurt his hand attempting a catch and as a result missed the following games against Northants and Middlesex. And by June of 1925 John had ceased to be a regular member of the Notts side.

The years had finally caught up with him. He was still physically strong. Eric says his father never trained but that he had an outstanding physique. He was by now though carrying a good deal of weight, a factor no doubt attributable to his diet. He loved traditional English food, especially roast beef with roast potatoes and peas washed down by ale and followed by treacle pudding, and in that sense at least he was solidly in the tradition of the great Alfred Mynn. It is said of the champion of Kent that when he came upon the young Will Caffyn drinking tea he reproved him with unaccustomed sternness. 'My boy,' he said, 'beef and beer are the things to play cricket on.' Challenged as to the suitability of such a diet, he thought for a moment. 'Well then,' he said, 'perhaps beer and beef.'

John Gunn would not have differed from Mynn's judgement. In the 1920s, however, he began to find himself required to sit for longer than was good for him in the company of one beer-drinker in particular. Not that he himself drank to excess. The problem was rather that there were times when he went short of sleep. The cause of his problem was his county captain.

At the time, A. W. Carr was comparatively young (he was born in 1893), single, ebullient, convivial. He owned a three-wheeler Morgan and he loved his drink. Unfortunately, not everyone in the Notts side was as much a toper. On away matches there would usually be a good deal of companionable drinking, although Wilf Payton, a life-long teetotaller, held himself aloof from such goings-on. But the rest of the side would often spend long evenings in a pub or hotel bar, accepting liquor from those inevitable hangers-on who wanted to be able to boast of having stood so-and-so such-and-such a drink. After which the team would return to their lodgings to sleep, often three to a bed, and try to be ready for next day's 'entertainment', as Charlie Harris always called it.

For John Gunn though, Carr was a problem. The Notts captain liked talking cricket over a pint of beer. After home matches his Morgan would usually be parked outside a Nottingham pub – the old Spread Eagle on Goldsmith Street was his favourite – and inside he would be talking, drinking and generally acting the part of hail fellow well met. On one occasion, indeed, he was so desperate to get to the Spread Eagle before closing time that he actually drove his Morgan up the pub's steps and attempted to steer it through the swing doors, where it not surprisingly became stuck. A large crowd gathered but Carr was in no sense abashed. 'Here, get this out,' he shouted to the startled onlookers, vaulting from the car and dashing into the pub, from where he re-emerged some few minutes later with crates of ale which he stacked into the back of his car before driving off into the night.

More often than not on occasions like this he would go to John Gunn's. Arriving at Holme Road, he would throw stones at the bedroom window where John and Grace had invariably retired to bed. 'Not that bugger again,' John would groan. Meanwhile Eric would have been summoned by Carr to help him in with the cases of beer. Carr regularly selected the easy-going John as his late-night drinking companion. So poor John would struggle into his clothes, mutter and curse his way downstairs, and keep Carr company until all the beer was consumed, which often took until three o'clock in the morning. At which point Carr would take himself off and John would stumble upstairs to try to snatch a last few hours sleep before the next day's cricket. 'He couldn't say no, you see,' Eric explained. 'Not because he wanted the drink, but because Carr was skipper and Dad was a player.'

We do not accuse Carr of deliberate bad behaviour. Far from it. Eric also recalls that although John and George both preferred A. O. Jones as a tactician they greatly admired Carr as someone who always stood by his players, and this view of him has been reinforced by our conversations with Willis Walker and Joe Hardstaff, both of whom spoke very warmly of Carr as a 'players' man'. Indeed, his wholehearted support of team members was eventually to cost him his captaincy, for in the famous row of 1934 he backed Bill Voce against the Notts committee, who supported the Australian tourists and Lancashire in their complaints that in bowling against them Voce had used 'unfair tactics'. Carr was an impeccable sportsman. In a letter to John Arlott, George Gunn recalls an occasion when Carr would not let Fred Barratt continue to bowl at Yorkshire because Fred had been doing what the Yorkshire bowlers had previously done to the Notts batsmen, deliberately scuffing up the wicket. 'It's not cricket,' Carr said, 'and I won't have it.'

No, at heart there was nothing wrong with Carr. The most one can accuse him of is a certain thoughtless, high-spirited quality in his make-up which led him to be indifferent to the normal cares of life. Once he nearly killed himself and five Nottinghamshire players when he swung his three-wheeler round a particularly sharp bend on the way back from Mansfield to Nottingham. 'He was on one wheel when he took that bend,' Eric recalled his father telling him.

The enforced late nights did not bring a premature end to John Gunn's career, though they cannot have helped. His great career was, in the course of things, coming to its close and the decline was rapid. In the 1922 season he was still being called upon to do a fair amount of bowling. He sent down 353 overs and took 38 wickets at a cost of 18.60 runs each, decidedly impressive figures. But his batting was still regarded as an essential part of the Notts success. True, his form in the 1922 season was disappointing and he finished with an average of only 26.37. Nevertheless, he scored two centuries, 110 against Glamorgan, 'an irreproachable innings,' according to the local paper, and 150 against Warwickshire, which the same paper described as 'not quite free from fault as he gave a chance at slip when 20' but which, that apart, was 'brilliant'. Sadly, his benefit match, against Yorkshire at Trent Bridge, was not a personal success. In the first innings he made only 10 and fared even worse in the second, being dismissed for 4. Another example, like his sole Test match in England, of the failure of his nerve on the really big occasion?

The following season he came second in the batting averages, with an aggregate of 1,173 runs and a final average of 37.83. *Wisden* remarked that the Notts batting that year was a model of consistency, and the phrase certainly applied to John Gunn. On 11 occasions he scored 40 or better, and in successive matches made 56 against Leicestershire, 42 and 25 not out against Derbyshire, 75 against Surrey (he and Whysall put on 138 in exactly two hours), 12 and 53 against Northants, 28 against Glamorgan and 59 against Middlesex. In a further sequence the same season he made 38 against Lancashire, 38 and 62 not out against Hampshire, 80 against Sussex, 36 and 65 against Worcestershire, 34 and 10 against Yorkshire, and 44 and 56 against Surrey at the Oval. In the season's final championship match he made 116 not out in the first innings against Essex at Leyton. 'Batting five hours and a quarter for his

John Gunn and his friend of longstanding, Wilfred Rhodes, photographed at John's Benefit match at Trent Bridge, 1922. Although he did little in the match itself, the size of the crowd must have pleased him.

first hundred of the season,' *Wisden* remarked, 'John Gunn showed his usual skill in meeting well-varied bowling that never became loose.' Alas, he was unable to finish the match because of an attack of lumbago. But his season's scores reveal what a force he continued to be. It would be the last time of which that could truly be said.

'On John Gunn's batting,' *Wisden* noted of the 1924 season, 'time told to some extent, his average going down from 37 to 26.' By John Gunn's own standards the 1924 season was not only a poor one, it implied an irreversible trend. For the first time since he had come into the county side, very nearly 30 years previously, he struggled. On eight occasions he passed 50 but in several matches he did next to nothing. Yet there were still moments when the flame burnt high. In the August match against Derbyshire, at Trent Bridge, he scored 76 and 52 not out, and the *Nottingham Evening Post* did no more than tell the truth when it remarked that he 'had a splendid match'. He also played a major part in one of the most remarkable games of that season, against Middlesex, also at Trent Bridge. Notts batted first and scored 462. 'On the first day,' *Wisden* records, 'John Gunn and Carr had a great partnership, putting on 196 before Gunn, owing to a strained leg, had for a time to retire.' He returned, however, and eventually scored 113. (George had earlier made 55.) When Middlesex batted they were all out for 253 and had to follow on. They did better in their second innings, managing 358, but even so it left Notts to score no more than 150 to win. George and Whysall put on 72 for the first wicket (George 38) at which point 'Gubby' Allen took over. He ran through the rest of the Notts batting, finishing with 6 for 31. Notts were all out for 122 (John Gunn 1) and Middlesex had won a famous victory. John, who had batted so magnificently in the first innings, can hardly be held accountable for the Notts defeat.

He was called on to bowl 203 overs in the season, and finished with 18 wickets at 25.38 each. He was no longer seen as a major strike bowler, and indeed had only been an irregular one since 1908 or 1909. His place in the side did not depend on his bowling. It did on his batting, however. And for all the heroics of his innings against Middlesex the string of low scores told its own tale.

So did other matters. Lumbago, a strained leg: the unmistakable signs of age. At the beginning of the 1925 season he was still included in the side, but he started disastrously. In the opening game, against Hampshire, he scored 18, and it was to prove his highest score for some time. The next match was against Sussex and he scored 11, followed by 2

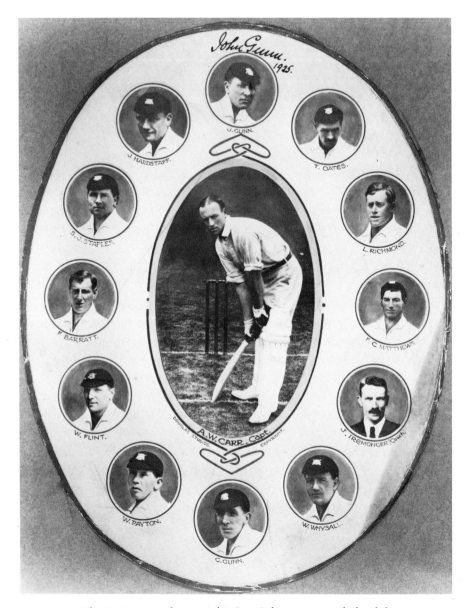

The Notts team of 1925, John Gunn's last season with the club.

against Derbyshire and then a meagre 7 in his one chance against Leicestershire.

The following match was the all-important Whitsuntide fixture against Surrey, for which Trent Bridge could guarantee a full house. But John Gunn was not in the side that went out to play against their old rivals. For the very first time since his apprentice days he had been dropped. As luck would have it the Surrey veteran bowler, Bill Hitch, was left out of the visitors' side. 'They sat on the balcony together,' Eric Gunn recalled, 'as miserable as sin.'

It is understandable. When you have given your life to the game you love it is not pleasant to have to admit that from now on it will continue without you. But so it was. John Gunn had ceased to command a regular place in the Notts side. Still, he was not quite finished. Early in July the team headed south, as it always did at that time of year, to play a trio of fixtures: against Kent, Sussex and Hampshire. On the last day of the Sussex game Wilf Payton was injured and the team had no adequate twelfth man. A telegram message was sent at short notice to John Gunn. 'Report Southampton.' But John was out when the messenger arrived. He had decided to celebrate his birthday – a little prematurely – with his friend Tom Underwood, and the pair had agreed to meet at the Spread Eagle. No doubt John was as keen on drowning his sorrows as congratulating himself on his 49th birthday. Certainly by the time Eric arrived with the news that he was needed at Southampton, his father was well into his cups. Eric had anticipated as much. He had put John's cricket gear and change of clothes into his car and driven post haste to the pub. There was just time to get him to the station for the last train south. 'All I can remember him saying,' Eric told us, 'is, "I'll show them if I'm finished, I'll show them."'

The following day Notts batted first and made 274, of which John's share was a careful, if undistinguished, 36. Hampshire replied with 348 and when Notts came out to bat again they soon lost George, and John joined Whysall at the crease. 'I'll show them, I'll show them,' he muttered as he took his guard. Some three hours later the pair had put on 208 runs, at which point Whysall was dismissed and George brought a drink out to his brother. 'What's up with you,' he said. 'Have you gone mad?' 'I'll show them if I'm finished,' John said, 'I'll show them.' He was eventually out for 166. He had shown them.

It was the last time he would do so. Great-hearted cricketer though he was he could not repair the slowing reflexes of his 49 years. On 1 August he played his last-ever game for the county. It was against Surrey, at the Oval, the same team and the same venue which had seen William Gunn's final game 21 years previously. John Gunn scored 39 and 25. As we shall see, he was by no means finished with cricket. But never again would he play for the county he had served with such unswerving dedication for so many years.

John Gunn did not attract the notice that was regularly directed towards his uncle and his brother. He had not the outstanding bearing of the one, nor did he possess the indefinable but authentic genius of the other. Yet in his own way he was a great professional. His career record, although it cannot tell us everything about him, tells us that much at least. He scored 23,194 runs for Notts, and only George has ever scored more for the county. He made 40 centuries, and again he is beaten into second place in this respect only by his brother. Time and again he performed with that mixture of resolve and flair that made him the most dependable of middle-order batsmen. He made big scores, but also innumerable fifties. If he did not like the quickest of bowling at least it can be said that he was never frightened by it; and against the less-than-best he could be destructively adventurous.

As for his bowling for Notts, he took 1,198 wickets at an overall average of 24.24 which, considering that he often had to do the donkey work and was also made to put in many a stint when officially past his best, is a remarkable achievement. He twice performed the hat-trick, first in 1899 then in 1904. And, as the Nottingham Evening Post pointed out, 'He was like magic in the field, particularly so at cover point.' He made no fewer than 215 catches for his county.

He may sound like the epitome of the journeyman cricketer, but a neighbour of his, Mrs Ann Coulthard, recalls that, neat and dapper as he always was – he invariably wore a dark suit and his trilby when going off to play cricket – he nevertheless had the instinct of an artist. He played the piano well, if not as well as George, and he sang beautifully. Whenever he went abroad he brought exquisite gifts back for his wife. It is fitting that his portrait, which now hangs in Trent Bridge, should have been painted by his grandson. Like his uncle, John was a great professional; but, like his brother, an unmistakable streak of artistry ran in his veins. Kindly, jolly, gregarious, an ideal family man; and beneath his bluff exterior sensitive of soul. In day-to-day affairs, quite as much as in cricket, John Gunn was a great allrounder.

10

'I LOVED YOU, GEORGE GUNN'

There are some cricketers who, when they have finished with the first-class game, decide to play no more. 'When you can play a bit,' Joe Hardstaff told us, 'you don't want someone making a cheap reputation by bowling you out on a cabbage patch.' But such cricketers are in the minority. The larger number prefer to drift gently down through local club cricket, or by playing in invitation XIs.

John Gunn was luckier than most. On his retirement he was 'hired' by Sir Julien Cahn, and became a general factotum to the furniture magnate. For Cahn had steadily built up the profitable furniture business which his father had left him and by the 1920s was rich enough to indulge himself as he pleased with his favourite activity – which was cricket. He had his own beautifully appointed private ground at Loughborough Road, Nottingham. (He would soon have a further delightful country-park ground at his house, Stanford Hall, near Loughborough.) He had his own team, which was as good as most county sides and regularly played top-class opposition, including the touring teams; and Cahn had un-limited admiration for good cricketers. When he hired John Gunn it was ostensibly as shop-walker for the Derby Road furniture store, but John's real duties lay elsewhere.

He was soon playing regularly for Cahn's XI. He also acted as coach; and occasionally he umpired. (When he was not needed in any of these capacities he turned out as professional for Retford, and in 1928 set a new club record when he finished with a batting average of 95.75.) In the latter half of the 1920s John played most of his cricket for Cahn, scoring over 4,000 runs (including five centuries) and taking some 170 wickets. At the end of the 1929 season he played for Cahn's XI against the South Africans and against Lancashire and the proceeds of both matches were given to him as a benefit.

John also spent much time in the nets, bowling to his employer. Sir Julien's talents as a cricketer were strictly limited and he was hampered by delicate bones, as a result of which he chose to wear a pair of specially made, inflatable pads. (They were strapped onto him and pumped up by his chauffeur, and Sir Julien was known often to dictate business affairs to his secretary while his chauffeur prepared him for an innings or a session in the nets.) Ken Wheatley, who as a lad in the 1930s knew John Gunn well, partly through his father, a well known butcher and cricket enthusiast, and partly because as a keen club cricketer he came into contact with him in the nets at Trent Bridge, described in a private letter John's 'quiet chuckle' as he told of how he would bowl to Sir Julien in the nets.

> I'd bowl very slowly to him. 'You're batting well this morning, Sir Julien,' I'd say. 'Do you think so, Gunn?' he'd reply. After a while, 'Well Gunn, there's five shillings on the wicket.' More bowling. 'My word, you *are* batting well, Sir Julien.' Sir Julien by now mighty pleased with himself. 'There's a pound on the stumps, Gunn.' Next three balls, bang, bang, bang, clean bowled every time. 'You must have lost your concentration, Sir Julien,' I'd say.

John told the young Ken Wheatley that he often made as much as £3 for his morning's work, which, as Mr Wheatley comments, 'wasn't a bad sum for those days.'

John was canny enough to know how to keep on the right side of Sir Julien. If he was umpiring and Sir Julien was batting it was no use the bowler appealing for leg-before, certainly not if Sir Julien had only just come to the wicket. More likely than not runs would be credited to the batsman as the ball ricocheted away off the inflated pads. '£13 a week and all found,' John explained to his son, Eric Gunn. 'You don't want to throw that away.'

Cahn's munificence was legendary. Many cricketers apart from John Gunn had reason to be grateful for his lavish hospitality and his abiding love of cricket. Early in 1930 he took a party to Argentina. It was the second tour he had organized, for early in 1929 he had taken a team to Jamaica. John joined the party, which sailed on the SS *Avalona Star*, initially as umpire, but he also played in some of the matches, and indeed scored 70 against the Argentina national team.

George was also abroad that winter. At an age when he might well have expected to spend the winter in grand idleness he was invited to be a member of the MCC party which toured West Indies under R. E. S. Wyatt. The tour was marked by beautiful weather and high scores. There were four Tests, two drawn, one victory to each side; and George finished fourth in the averages, with 34.50. His individual scores in the Tests were: 35 and 29, 1 and 23, 11 and 45, 85 and 47. His habit of walking down the wicket by turns infuriated and bewildered the West Indian bowlers who as a result bowled persistently short to him; and the local press described him as 'the man who walks down the pitch and tickles them where he likes.' He also won over the crowds. Frank Stokes told us

◄ ● ►

George Gunn and Bill Voce off to the West Indies, 14 December 1929. Among the party giving them a send-off at the Nottingham Midland station are James Iremonger, John Gunn and Sam Staples (between Bill Voce and George with pipe); Harold Larwood (with cigarette) and Ben Lilley (far right).

that, when the West Indians were batting, George would enjoy himself if two of their batsmen were having a mid-wicket conference by creeping towards them with pantomimic caution, hand cocked to ear. 'He's comin', he hear you,' the crowd would yell. Whereupon George would put a finger to his lips and tiptoe elaborately away. George's highest score of that happy tour was 178 against Jamaica, when he and Sandham put on 322 for the first wicket. And, an added bonus, Wyatt succeeded in teaching him to swim.

It may seem surprising that a man in his fifty-first year was asked to go on tour. But George was there on merit. He was still one of the finest batsmen in the country. In 1926, when Notts finished fourth in the championship, George came third in the county averages, with 1,177 runs from 33 innings. A broken little finger in the game against Lancashire kept him out of the side for 13 matches, otherwise he might well have done better. As it was he scored 114 against Sussex, made 191 in the Whitsuntide game against Surrey, and against Gloucestershire carried his bat for 67 through the first innings (the fifth time in his career that he had accomplished this feat) and scored 68 in the second.

The following season Notts all but won the championship. Indeed, until near the end of the season they seemed certain of the prize. Then they ran out of luck. Larwood had wrenched his knee in a Test trial match at Bristol and could play no more, and Carr went down with a bad cold. For the last three games of the season Notts called up Lionel Kirk, who was captain of the Second XI. As the team waited at the station for the train that was to take them to Glamorgan, their opponents in the final, crucial match, so one story goes, a representative of the Notts committee rushed up to offer George the captaincy, but George turned it down by saying, 'This is too important to be left to a professional.' However that may be, the match was a disaster for Notts, who had only to draw it to make sure of the championship. Glamorgan hadn't won a county game all season and when Notts batted first and scored 233, of which George's contribution was 68, there was no reason for a Notts supporter to fear that anything untoward was about to happen. But Lilley injured himself, Whysall was forced to take over as wicketkeeper and let through 23 byes, catches were dropped and Glamorgan led on first innings by 142 runs. When Notts batted again they lost two quick wickets, including George's, before play ended on the second day. Overnight there was much rain, then next morning the sun appeared and the remaining eight wickets went down for 38 runs. Notts had lost by an innings and with their defeat went the championship. George and Whysall travelled straight from Glamorgan to Folkestone, to play in a festival match. The rest of the disconsolate party had to return to face the wrath of their supporters.

The loss of the championship was clearly a fearful disappointment. Yet George had no reason to feel dissatisfied with his own season. He scored over 1,600 runs, for the third time in his career made centuries in both innings of a match (against Warwickshire), made a further hundred against Gloucestershire; and *Wisden* commented that 'To George Gunn, thanks to his finished style and clever footwork, run getting seemed to come as easily as it did twenty years ago.'

In 1928 Notts finished third in the championship. Their bowling was now impressive in both depth and variety. Larwood was fit again, Fred Barratt was still bowling fast and well (that season, in fact, he did the double, the first Notts player to have done so since John Gunn in 1906), there was Sam Staples to bowl spin and also the 19-year-old Bill Voce, who was as yet often used as an off-break bowler and who was beginning to keep 'Tich' Richmond out of the side. Richmond in fact had begun to play regularly for Cahn's team, and was to collect over 700 wickets in the ten years he turned out for Sir Julien.

The batting was equally impressive in strength. The only doubt had to do with the ages of several of the batsmen. George was approaching 50, Payton was nearly 47 and Whysall had turned 41. Yet still they topped the averages. And as *Wisden* remarked, 'George Gunn lives as one of the cricketing marvels of the age. No man has ever made batting look more simple than this veteran, and his genius was almost as pronounced as during the earlier stages of his career. He played a wonderful innings to beat Kent at Trent Bridge, and besides that memorable 100 not out, he reached three figures upon five other occasions, the graceful ease of his methods being just as striking as it had been twenty years previously.'

Fittingly enough, George's first century that season was 122 against Surrey in the Whitsuntide game, a match in which his old friend Jack Hobbs scored the 150th century of his career. Then came the first of his two centuries against Kent, in which 'Gunn drove and cut brilliantly, scoring 115 out of 169 in three hours.' In late June the county scored 656 for 3 against Warwickshire. George scored 148, his partner Whysall 132, and their first-wicket partnership, which lasted three hours, realised 245 runs. Against Northants George made 159 in the second innings (it was the fiftieth century of his career), and against Hampshire at Bournemouth he and Willis Walker scored 265 in just over three hours (Walker 156, George 144). Finally came the wonderful innings against Kent at Trent Bridge. Everyone who saw George bat that day seems to agree that it would be impossible to imagine a finer example of the skills and beauty of the batsman's art. Notts were set 157 to win in two hours and a quarter. In fact they got the runs in an hour and 35 minutes. Whysall helped George to put on 148 for the first wicket, George reaching his sixth century of the season. Perhaps we shouldn't be surprised that the impression George left seems incommunicable. 'It wasn't that he did anything out of the ordinary,' one person told us, adding: 'No, I don't mean that. I mean that he didn't take any chances and he didn't seem even to make an effort. But they couldn't bowl to him, that was all. They tried everything, but he just kept scoring.'

In 1929 Notts finally managed to win the championship. It was the first time since 1907 that they had done so. In *Cricket With the Lid Off*, A. W. Carr wrote of the season that 'the majority of us were on top of our form and what helped us enormously was that four of our bowlers, Barratt, Sam Staples, Larwood and Voce all took more than 100 wickets each . . . And five of us scored more than 1,000 runs . . . George Gunn hit his 1,000 and so did Wilfred Payton, Walker, Whysall and myself.' So bare a rehearsal of the figures disguises the extraordinary achievements of that summer, and especially those of George. Not that he finished top of the averages, for that honour went to Whysall. But as *Wisden* noted, George's batting during 1929 was undoubtedly remarkable for a man who in June passed his fiftieth birthday. Altogether that summer he scored 1,788 runs for the county, including four centuries, two against Sussex (in one of which, at Eastbourne, he carried his bat through the innings for the seventh time in his career), one against Glamorgan, when he scored 178, and, most wonderful of all, 164 not out against Worcestershire, on his fiftieth birthday.

A short while after Notts had made sure of the championship, George gave an interview to the *Nottingham Guardian*, in which he said that as one of the only two players who had played in the previous championship team of 1907 – the other being Wilf Payton – he did not wish to compare the two sides.

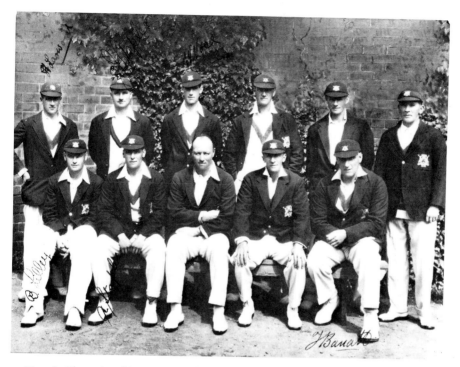

*Notts's Championship-winning side of 1929. Left to right, standing: H. Larwood,
S. J. Staples, W. Voce, W. W. Whysall, W. Walker, W. R. D. Payton; sitting,
B. Lilley, A. Staples, A. W. Carr, G. Gunn, F. Barratt.*

Conditions then were vastly different. It was a rainy season and the
wickets were not covered, whereas this year we have enjoyed a dry
summer . . . The struggle, particularly during the last few matches, has
been terrific. There is no doubt that in the position in which we have
been placed we have not been able to play our natural game. As a rule
we play happy-go-lucky cricket which is the best policy to pursue. But,
like every county on the verge of the county championship, we have had
to mind our Ps and Qs. I perhaps have more reason than anyone to be
pleased with what we have done, because at the age of fifty I have gone
through the season, playing in every match.

Nor was the season over. On Saturday, 14 September Notts began a
four-day match as county champions against the Rest of England. The
Rest had an extremely strong side. In batting order it read: Hobbs,

Surrey County Cricket Club

KENNINGTON OVAL

CHAMPION COUNTY v. REST OF ENGLAND

SATURDAY, SEPT. 14th, 1929. (Four-Day Match)

REST OF ENGLAND.

	First Innings		Second Innings	
1 Hobbs (Surrey)	c Larwood, b Barratt ...	2	b Bland ...	68
2 Sandham (Surrey)	c Gunn (G), b Larwood	82	lbw, b Larwood ...	15
3 Woolley (Kent)	b Barratt ...	106	c Whysall, b Staples ...	15
4 O'Connor (Essex)	c Bland, b Larwood ...	6	c Gunn (V), b Bland ...	10
* 5 R. E. S. Wyatt (Warwickshire)	c Barratt, b Staples ...	85	b Barratt ...	11
6 Leyland (Yorkshire)	c Whysall, b Bland ...	17	c & b Bland ...	75
† 7 Ames (Kent)	c Whysall, b Staples ...	15	b Barratt ...	0
8 R. W. V. Robins (Middlesex)	b Bland ...	37	st Lilley, b Staples ...	46
9 Tate (Sussex)	c Carr, b Bland ...	32	c Whysall, b Staples ...	7
10 Goddard (Gloucestershire)	b Larwood ...	13	not out ...	13
11 Clark (Northamptonshire)	not out ...		c Lilley, b Staples ...	16
	B 1, l-b 2, w , n-b ...	3	B 2, l-b 5, w , n-b ...	7
	Total ...	**399**	**Total** ...	**282**

FALL OF THE WICKETS

1-5	2-159	3-170	4-209	5-244	6-272	7-337	8-383	9-397
1-31	2-77	3-105	4-114	5-135	6-135	7-242	8-245	9-260

BOWLING ANALYSIS

	First Innings						Second Innings					
	O.	M.	R.	W.	Wd.	N-b.	O.	M.	R.	W.	Wd.	N-b.
Larwood	18	3	54	3			15	1	73	1		
Barratt	21	1	83	2			18	2	50	2		
Staples	36.1	7	146	2			18.5	2	63	4		
Bland	24	2	106	3			13	0	75	3		
Gunn (G. V.)	2	0	7	0			2	0	14	0		

CHAMPION COUNTY (NOTTS).

	First Innings		Second Innings	
1 Gunn (G.)	b Tate ...	8	b Robins ...	96
2 Whysall	b Clark ...	97	c O'Connor, b Goddard ...	50
3 Walker	c Tate, b Clark ...	1	c Sandham, b Robins ...	0
* 4 A. W. Carr	b Woolley ...	91	b Goddard ...	6
5 Payton	c Ames, b Clark ...	21	c Hobbs, b Robins ...	32
† 6 Lilley	c Tate, b Clark ...	10	b Goddard ...	5
8 Barratt	c Wyatt, b Woolley ...	54	c Sandham, b Clark ...	45
10 Gunn (G. V.)	st Ames, b Robins ...	6	lbw, b Robins ...	17
9 Staples (S.)	lbw, b Robins ...	21	not out ...	18
11 Larwood	st Ames, b Robins ...	11	c Woolley, b Robins ...	11
5 R. D. F. Bland	not out ...	15	c Woolley, b Robins ...	1
	B 17, l-b 10, w , n-b 2 ...	29	B 14, l-b 13, w , n-b 1 ...	28
	Total ...	**364**	**Total** ...	**309**

FALL OF THE WICKETS

1-21	2-35	3-204	4-229	5-256	6-265	7-300	8-336	9-339
1-88	2-114	3-122	4-141	5-200	6-209	7-271	8-279	9-299

BOWLING ANALYSIS

	First Innings						Second Innings					
	O.	M.	R.	W.	Wd.	N-b.	O.	M.	R.	W.	Wd.	N-b.
Clark	25	5	68	4		2	25	5	73	1		1
Tate	21	2	64	1			13	4	38	0		
Goddard	14	2	52	0			23	5	56	3		
Robins	26.1	6	108	3			27.3	3	89	6		
Woolley	9	0	42	2			4	0	12	0		
Wyatt							4	0	13	0		

* Captain.
† Wkt.-keeper.
Umpires—Hardstaff and Stone.

Toss won by Rest of England.
Hours of Play—11.30 a.m. till 5.30 p.m.   Luncheon 1.30
RESULT—Rest of England won by 8 runs.

A silk scorecard of the Notts v Rest of England match, 1929.

Sandham, Woolley, O'Connor, Wyatt, Leyland, Ames, Robins, Tate, Goddard and Clark. The Rest batted first and made 399, of which Woolley's 106 was the outstanding feature. Notts replied with 364 (Whysall 97, Carr 91) and when the Rest batted again they scored 282, leaving Notts to score 318 to win. George and Whysall began the county's second innings on Tuesday evening and had put on 88 when Whysall was caught by O'Connor off the bowling of Goddard for 50. At close of play Notts were 99 for 1. On the last day Walker and Carr went cheaply, but Payton stayed and Barratt hit powerfully as the score edged nearer the required total. And George? He simply shut up one end. *Wisden* remarked that he displayed 'such superb defence and unlimited patience that a win for his side and a personal triumph in the shape of a three-figure innings would have been a fitting reward for his skill.' Sadly, it was not to be. When he had reached 96 he was bowled by Robins. He was eighth out at 279 and he had given Notts a wonderful chance of winning the match. But although Staples and Larwood did their best the last wicket fell at 309, leaving Notts nine short of their target. It had been a great game of cricket and the *Daily Mail* rightly remarked that 'Towering above all else in the day's play and, indeed, in the match, was the performance of George Gunn.' His 96 runs had taken him four hours 25 minutes and he had not given a chance. If you set that innings beside the 100 against Kent you have some measure of the man's comprehensive genius. Whether in attack or in defence George Gunn was one of the greatest batsmen of all time.

George may have been disappointed by the outcome of that final match, but otherwise the season had brought him immense pleasure. There had been the thrill of winning the championship and of the team's formal reception by and presentation to the Lord Mayor of Nottingham. And there had been his fiftieth birthday celebrations at Trent Bridge. As their way of honouring George, the Notts committee organized a presentation during the tea interval of the first day's play against Worcestershire at Trent Bridge. George was given a mahogany drawing-room clock and Flo, who was, as so often, present to watch him play, received a silver trinket box. Carr gave George a silver cigarette case, and his team-mates presented him with a gold wrist watch. A large crowd had gathered outside the pavilion as the presentations were made and burst spontaneously into 'For He's a Jolly Good Fellow'. George then spoke. He thanked the club and his team-mates for their presents and said that,

A studio portrait of George Gunn taken on his fiftieth birthday when he scored his memorable 164 not out against Worcestershire.

A. W. Carr presenting gifts to George from himself and the players in honour of his fiftieth birthday.

'Had it not been for the generosity of a few members of the committee in 1906 . . . I should not be playing for the county at fifty years of age. My relations with members of the committee have always been most happy, and if I had my time to come again, I don't know that I should choose anything different.'

Fred Root was playing for Worcestershire in that match and, in *A Cricket Pro's Lot*, he recalls that after the presentations George 'came out to bat visibly affected by all the good and sincere things that had been said about him. He played a wretched shot at the very first ball I bowled to him, and was out to a "dolly" catch at short leg. Poor "Dodger" Whysall was almost as sorry as myself about this happening, and the feelings of the crowd could be sensed in the middle. If ever I felt like calling a batsman back it was on that occasion.'

Fred Root's feelings do him credit for on a very recent previous occasion he would have done a great deal to have got George out. On the eve of George's birthday Notts were playing Worcestershire at Worcester and stayed – as they always did – at a hotel down by the river. Jimmy Haynes, who at that time made a living from the sale of cricket gear, dabbled in theatrical entertainments, played good local cricket, was on the umpires list, and followed Notts cricket, was present on that occasion. He followed the team literally, doing his best to make sure that business trips took him to wherever the team happened to be playing. On 12 June he arrived at the team's hotel at tea-time and George immediately sent him into town to buy some sheet music from a well known music shop. 'It's my birthday tomorrow' George told him, 'so tonight we're going to have a bit of a sing-song.'

After supper the players crowded round the piano, the hotel proprietress – 'a very nice lady' – provided sandwiches, jugs of beer were brought, and the sing-song began. George played selections from 'Iolanthe', 'Watchman what of the Night' and much else beside, everyone else sang, more beer was brought, further supplies of sandwiches consumed, midnight came and went, and the team eventually staggered off to bed as the sun came up.

A few hours later a sore-headed bunch of cricketers met for breakfast and then began the walk along the riverpath to the ground. Groans and moans. 'Oh, I do feel awful,' Jimmy remembers someone saying.

'Do you?' George said, turning round to him. 'You ought to be like Wilf here,' nodding towards Wilf Payton, 'he's as right as rain.' Wilf Payton, who was a life-long teetotaller, agreed.

'And I'm surprised you're not feeling it at your age, George,' he said.

'I'm feeling a treat,' George – who had been 16 not out overnight – said. 'In fact I think I'll score a hundred today.' And on his fiftieth birthday that is precisely what he did. Worcestershire tried all their bowlers, including of course Fred Root, who George always said gave him more trouble than any English bowler except Astill of Leicestershire; but it made no difference. Jimmy Haynes recalls that in the middle of the afternoon, when George was well past his hundred, Worcestershire's captain, Major M. F. S. Jewell, took off Tarbox, who had had a long bowl, and threw the ball to Fred Root, meaning to give him another chance. Fred said something to his captain and threw it back. 'What did he say?' Jimmy asked George at tea, by which time George had reached 164 not out.

'He said, "I'm not bowling to that old bugger again,"' George told him.

As Jimmy Haynes came to the end of telling this story he was clearly torn between laughter and tears. 'I *loved* you, George Gunn,' he exclaimed.

Although George failed in his 'presentation' innings at Trent Bridge, the Gunn cause was upheld by his son, George Vernon, who made 73. G.V. or 'young George' had been on the club's books since 1926, had played a few games in 1928 and by 1929 was beginning to establish himself as a fairly regular member of the county side. (He played in the match against the Rest of England.) A loveable, eternally optimistic cricketer, young George hoped and tried to emulate his father. Unfortunately, he could not manage to do so. Joe Hardstaff reckoned that 'George Vernon was a very good county cricketer, but he wanted to play the kind of shots "Poppa" [G.V.'s name for his father] played. And he couldn't. Nobody could.' Presumably his understandable if hopeless ambition began to affect his form, for in 1930 G.V. played only seven matches for Notts, finishing with an average of 20.09. 'If he was half as good as he thinks he is, he'd be twice as good as he is,' George wryly remarked.

By contrast, George played another full season and finished fourth in the county averages. *Wisden* remarked that 'George Gunn did great things for a man of 51.' Perhaps his finest achievement that season was a superb innings against Kent, when he scored 129 out of 190 made in two hours, including seventeen fours. He also made a century against Glamorgan.

That season, however, the Notts committee had offered him a carefully worded contract.

> For the sum of £100 paid in twelve monthly instalments, the services of the said George Gunn shall be retained by the Committee of the Nottinghamshire Club to play for the county when and where required. At the same time George Gunn shall be free to join any league cricket club he may desire, providing the above clause is involved in any agreement made with such a club.

Sir Julien Cahn could have had no thoughts about replacing George's older brother. In 1930 John Gunn topped the batting averages for Cahn's XI, with 60.00 from 480 runs, and that included a century against Essex in September.

In the early winter of 1930 poor Whysall died. He fell while at a dance in Mansfield, cut his elbow, and what at first seemed a minor injury turned into septicaemia. He died on 11 November. He had been George's opening partner in no fewer than 41 century partnerships, and it may be that his death persuaded the Notts committee that the time for change had now come. At all events, they used the 1931 season to introduce new, young players. George and Wilf Payton were dropped for the opening matches. A month later, when none of the opening partnerships tried had proved a success, George was back. Walter Hammond remembers, in *Cricket My World*, 'the looks and words of relief when it was learned definitely that "old George" had dropped out of big cricket; and then the "words" that echoed from Somerset to Yorkshire when the retired veteran was recalled.'

He returned with a third of the season already over. By the time it came to an end he had scored 1,329 runs, with what *The Cricketer* described as 'a wonderful 117 against Lancashire, and 183 at Edgbaston, whilst he gave the New Zealanders a three figure demonstration of what batting should be, besides admirably leading the side in the absence of his captain.' The same journal also praised young George.

> G. V. Gunn, having rid himself of early over-confidence, looks like making a glorious player. To this critic [Sir Home Gordon] his play is reminiscent of the early delightful methods of the late V. F. S. Crawford . . . It is delightful to see the old names in the new generation of players: Gunn, Hardstaff and Oates. May they all do as well as their forebears. George Vernon Gunn had an average of 29 and scored his first championship century.

That first century came at Edgbaston. And it so happens that during the same innings his father scored 183. It is a unique feat in first-class cricket for a father and son to score centuries in the same innings. Yet young George very nearly did not make it. According to the *Nottingham Guardian*:

> when Notts passed Warwickshire's total at a quarter past six, after Carr had claimed the optional half hour to enable the first innings to be decided, the colt had scored 95 and the umpires and the home players were preparing to leave the field. Harris, who was Gunn's junior partner in the great stand which put Notts on top, approached Wyatt, the Warwickshire captain, with a request that he should give his colleague a chance of getting his first hundred. The spectators, without knowing what was happening in the middle, lent unconscious support to the play by shouting 'go on, go on,' and Wyatt, acquiescing, beckoned to Santall to take the ball. Off the over Gunn took four, three of which came from an overthrow. Bates went on at the other end and Gunn got a single to complete his hundred out of 153 in two hours and twenty minutes.

Of George's innings against the New Zealand tourists, the same newspaper remarked that, apart from giving a sharp chance when he was on 86, the 'father of the Notts team never put his bat wrong until he had completed 100 out of 203 in a trifle over three and a half hours . . . his batting was splendid and eleven 4s introduced nearly every shot in the book.' The New Zealanders had cause to remember the Gunns. For when they played Cahn's XI later that season, in a match to raise money for Whysall's widow, the 55-year-old John Gunn — who else? — took a century off them.

Notts finished fifth in the table, a position which would undoubtedly have been higher but for the fact that several of them had to spend some time in hospital. The team was returning from a drawn match at Leicester. Heading the convoy was a lorry containing the team's equipment and driven by young George; behind him came Larwood's car, containing besides Larwood himself, Sam Staples and Ben Lilley; and behind them came the rest of the side, in a variety of motor vehicles. Coming into Nottingham, young George somehow overturned the lorry, Larwood ran into the back of it, and he and the other occupants were thrown out. Larwood, G. V. and Staples all missed the next match.

However, young George was fit and well at the beginning of the next season, as was his father. But 1932 was to mark the end of George's career as a first-class cricketer. The season began splendidly. Notts's first match was against Sussex, and on 9 May the *Nottingham Guardian* reported as follows:

> George Gunn, who will be 53 next month, was reported to have had less than half an hour's practice prior to the day of the match, but to have stated that if he could survive the first three overs he would be quite alright. The chance to substantiate his claim came straight away, for A. W. Carr won the toss and sent the veteran in to open the innings with Keeton. With the first ball sent down, a poor length delivery from Tate just outside the off stump, Gunn was as much at home again as though he had been batting every day for weeks. The four which rewarded a characteristic cut brought all the confidence needed, and during the next hour and forty minutes the 'man who never grows old' gathered 67 of the 132 produced by a wonderful first wicket stand. There was poetry in every stroke that Gunn played, a negligent audacity contrasting sharply with the no less accurate but sterner hitting of Keeton . . . The veteran had reached the stage when he was beginning to walk out to the bowling, but in the end one of Jim Langridge's left-arm slows encompassed his downfall. Gunn tried to turn the ball to leg, was too late, and a leg before appeal terminated a superb innings which included one 6 and eight 4s.

Then came a trial match at Trent Bridge which saw George Gunn captaining a side that included both his sons. For in addition to young George, John Stapleton 'Jack' Gunn also played. According to the *Nottingham Guardian*, Jack Gunn, who took one for 32 off nine overs and whose repertoire included the googly, 'is a tall well-built youth, who may eventually add to the traditions of an illustrious family.'

Whether Jack ever intended to take up cricket seriously is doubtful. Yet his father told Frank Stokes that if Jack had persisted he would have become a better cricketer than G.V. As it was, the younger boy did not go onto the Notts books and soon left the area. He became a successful businessman and died in March 1983, leaving a widow, a son and a daughter.

A few days after the trial match Notts were to play Surrey in the Whitsuntide game. The Surrey team always stayed at the Black Boy Hotel in Nottingham's Market Square and the night before the game George called in at the hotel. According to one version he was there to be

Father and sons. George with George Vernon on his left and Jack on his right on the occasion of the Trent Bridge Trial match, 1932.

measured for a suit, according to another he had simply come for a drink with some of the Surrey players who, if they were to be opponents on the following day, were still his friends and, in several cases, companions of many years. What seems to be agreed is that he overheard them discussing how to get him out. Albert Underwood, an umpire who was later to stand with George in war-time matches and who knew him well, believes George heard Alf Gover declare, 'Well, if I can't bowl him out I'll have to knock him out.'

The next day Notts won the toss and in poor light George went out to open the Notts innings with Keeton. According to the *Nottingham Guardian*:

A. Gover, Surrey's big fast bowler finished his long run up to the crease, the ball appeared to slip out of his hand and a full toss hurtled head high at Gunn who failed in an attempt to turn it to leg and was struck violently on the right side of the face just against the eye. Dropping his bat, the veteran reeled away from the crease with both hands clasped to his head and was falling as Brooks the Surrey stumper, Gover and Keeton rushed to render assistance. Laid gently on the grass he was attended to by Dr W. F. Neil and then escorted to the pavilion. Examination at the hospital showed no bones were broken and the patient was returned home with instructions to rest quietly for three or four days.

There can be no suggestion that the horrified Gover meant to hit George. The remark of the previous evening had been made in jest. His distress at having hit George was genuine, as was the distress of most of his team-mates. It was not, possibly, shared by his captain. According to one source, Jardine stood by unmoved while George was attended to and 'Get him off the field' was his only comment.

George was out of the side until 25 June, when he returned against Gloucestershire and scored 58. He missed the next match against Leicestershire but played against Derbyshire, scoring 75 in the first innings, by 'fine cricket', and 1 in the second. Then the Indians came to Trent Bridge. The *Nottingham Guardian* for 4 July reported that 'the story of the fate which overtook the home side could be dated from the early dismissal of George Gunn, who usually shines against fast bowling but who had no relish for Amar Singh's deliveries, which flashed off the pitch. He was caught at slip with only one run scored.' In the second innings he managed 20, was again caught at slip, and that was his last game for Nottinghamshire. Perhaps fittingly, John Gunn also played his last first-class game at about the same time, for Sir Julien Cahn's XI against the South Americans at Loughborough Road.

With the possible exception of Alfred Mynn, it is difficult to believe that there has ever been a more widely loved cricketer than George Gunn. That he was a genius there can be no doubt. He was also *sui generis*. Nobody could play like him and he was absolutely his own man. Perhaps that explains why he fell out with his uncle and why he chose to use Britain's Best bats, rather than the Gunn & Moore favoured by the rest of the Notts side. 'What's that bit of old planking you've got there?' he would ask a batsman coming to join him at the wicket, as soon as he made out the Gunn & Moore label.

His humour was whimsical, never vicious. Joe Hardstaff – who came into the Notts side in George's last seasons – tells of how George would wander about the changing-room at Trent Bridge: 'He'd put his trousers on one peg, his shirt on another, his shoes somewhere else. And if he was playing against a no-hope bowler he'd come in and tell us "that lad'll play for England". Whereas if it was Tate he'd say "can't bowl for toffee". We never knew whether to believe him – he always kept a straight face.'

And he recalls a piece of advice George offered him and the young Charlie Harris at Liverpool. At the end of the day's play Joe and Charlie were talking about the girls they were going to go after that evening. 'George called us over,' Joe said, 'and we went a bit sheepish, because of all our bragging.

"That game you two reckon you're going to go playing," he said to them.

"Yes?" Charlie Harris asked.

"Just remember, it's the only game that the more you practise the wuss you get. Think on't." ' So at least the tale goes.

Hardstaff clearly loved George. 'I remember when I was new in the side,' he said. 'We were on a sticky down at Bristol and old Charlie Parker was bowling. I couldn't lay a bat on him. So I went down the wicket at the end of an over and said to George, "I'm sorry, Mr Gunn, but I don't like this."

"Don't you worry," he said, "leave him to me." And,' Joe added wonderingly, 'he played him for half an hour until I got my bearings and he made him look *easy*. The ball never got away from the middle of his bat.'

He revelled in remembering George's waywardness, his ability to frustrate, bewilder and outwit bowlers. 'He'd got two shots to every ball,' Joe said. 'A bowler'd bowl him, say, a goodish ball just on off stump and old George now, he'd play it back up the pitch and nod very gravely. So the bowler'd think "well I'd best keep it there or thereabouts". Next ball would pitch on exactly the same spot and it would go straight back past him or through the covers for four. And George would just look at the bowler as though he hadn't seen him before.'

In *A Cricket Pro's Lot* Fred Root wrote that George,

> would walk up the wicket to all sorts of bowling and finally play a correct shot with the utmost ease. Always seemed to be off his balance, but seldom was inconvenienced by this strange strolling habit of his. 'Steered' the ball with safety through the slips, and was a past-master of the leg glide. Adept at stealing singles, his grand judgement enabled him actually to trot runs where less knowledgeable players would have had to bustle . . . Of the many players I have bowled against, George was the most difficult to get out.

And for good measure he adds that,

> George was the best player of fast bowling I ever saw. When Arnold Warren was at his very best for Derbyshire, he would turn round to me and say, 'I simply can't bowl at George. He makes me look so slow, that I'm rapidly becoming qualified to apply for a pall-bearer's job at a funeral.' All speed merchants were made to look the same when George Gunn was opposed to them.

In 1936 Cecil Parkin published his *Cricket Triumphs and Troubles*, in which he paid his own tribute to George's greatness as a player of fast bowling.

> Even McDonald didn't like bowling against him – the only batsman of whom 'Mac' stood in awe. George was a heart-breaker. He used to walk forward to meet the ball as the bowler started to bowl, and as he walked he smiled and shouted, 'come on, it's all right.' If ever there was anything calculated to put a bowler off that was it, and many a bowler has stopped his run, gone back to his mark and started again because of George's little saunter up the pitch. But to McDonald he used to call 'Come on, Mac, I'll tame you!'

Ken Wheatley wrote that his father told him that 'All the Gunns had the sight or vision of an eagle. Dad told me that when Jack [John Gunn] was young he could catch a fly between forefinger and thumb. I was with Dad once when he said to George, "George, why did you have so much time in which to play your shots?"

George replied, "Bert, all I can tell you is that the *instant* the ball leaves the bowler's hand I know exactly where it's going to pitch."'

His eyesight served him well when he was playing against his old adversary, Fred Root. Once, Root bowled him with a ball that came in from the off. A perfect googly, everyone said. But George knew it wasn't. Afterwards, he challenged Fred, 'That wasn't a googly, was it?'

'No,' Root admitted, 'it hit something.' George told this story to Frank Stokes, who asked him how he knew.

'I could see the way it was spinning in the air,' George said. His sight was so keen that he did not have to bother to 'read' the bowler's action.

It was this 'eagle vision' that probably also explained George's abilities as a fielder. Even in his last season he was picking up his regular quota of slip catches and Grahame Booker remembers that his 'fielding was as whimsical as his batting . . . I recall one-handed catches plucked out of the air with nonchalant ease.' It was a trait that young George attempted to follow, often with disastrous results. For where son was a good, average cricketer, father was, as Robertson-Glasgow puts it, a character of 'eccentric individuality, wit and humour'.

In *Good Days*, Neville Cardus, a passionate admirer of George's, called him 'the wittiest batsman that ever lived . . . He played the game for fancy's sake; he never knew where the imp of his genius was going to take him.' And Cardus reports that often when sauntering a single, 'he would pat the turf with his bat'. He also took middle-stump guard, but only to check the chances of being lbw, since he never bothered to put his bat down where he had made his mark.

In *Cricket My World* Walter Hammond calls George 'this prince of batsmen,' and in *Cricket My Destiny* writes that 'Macartney, George Gunn and Don Bradman bracket for top places in my mind as the supreme batsmen of the 1919–39 era.' That is praise indeed, although as we have seen it is matched by the views of Jessop and Hobbs.

If George did not play as many times for England as he undoubtedly should have done we may put that down partly to what Jessop contemptuously referred to as 'paper form', for, as again everyone agrees, George got himself out on many occasions when he couldn't be bothered to stay in. But Warner and the 'Lord's circle' must take a good deal of the blame. Warner's curious explanation for George's falling into official disfavour – that he 'stood too much in front of his wicket' – does not bear close inspection, as all the great players who played against him were ready to testify.

Did George care that his unique abilities were so often and unjustly overlooked? It is impossible to know. Joe Hardstaff thinks not. 'No, he wouldn't have bothered, leastways I don't think so. He'd rather go his own way than do what others told him. Of course,' he added, 'it's true that you've got to be twice as good north of Watford as south of it if you're going to get in the England team.' But George was twice as good, wasn't he?, we asked. 'Twice?' Joe exclaimed. 'Nobody could touch him. He were a genius. A bloody genius.'

11
INTO
RETIREMENT

At the beginning of the 1933 season there was only one Gunn still playing first-class cricket. G.V. was by now an established member of the Notts side, and although never an outstanding player he was unfailingly loyal, capable and enthusiastic. 'Didn't matter if he'd had a bad run himself,' Joe Hardstaff told us, who spoke warmly about young George. 'He'd say "Who're we playing next then?" And when he was told who it'd be, "Oh, poor old . . ." whoever it was. "We'll see to *them*." '

You could not dim young George's passion for the game, nor his belief in himself. It was, of course, a somewhat inflated belief. There are numerous stories of his attempts to imitate 'poppa', and people who saw him say, 'If he'd been as good as he thought he was he'd have been one of the best.' Grahame Booker remembers G.V. 'fielding at mid-off, reaching lazily for a dolly catch with one hand. Well, dad used to do it. The only difference was that G.V. dropped it!'

Still, cricket was his livelihood, and he needed it. In 1926 he had married Renee Tyler Sheasby. Her parents kept the Trent Bridge Inn, from where, of course, Notts cricket, under the powerful influence of 'Old' Clarke, may be said to have begun. Inevitably Notts cricketers would call in for a drink there and that was no doubt how George and Renee met. Once married, the pair went to live with George and Flo at Albert Road and there, in August 1927, a son, George Vernon David, was born. Soon afterwards the young family moved to a house on Musters Road, also in West Bridgford. In August 1932, Renee gave birth to a daughter, christened Pauline Ann, and two years later, again in August, the third and final child was born. He was called Michael John. Pauline Manders, as she now is, remembers that her grandparents took a great interest in their three grandchildren and that they 'spoilt' her in particular. They also arranged for her to go 'to a "Miss Bissell's School for Young Ladies" when I was four years old.' The Bissell in question will

George Vernon and Renee on honeymoon.

◆ ● ●

have been a daughter of that sister of William Gunn's, to whom the Nottingham Giant left a house in West Bridgford.

While the children were being educated, their father was playing cricket. In his early years with the club, G.V. seems to have been used as an allrounder. Perhaps there were hopes he would develop into another John Gunn. In 1932 he played in 27 matches, scored 774 runs at an average of 24.97 and took 14 wickets at a cost of 17.07 each. He bowled right-arm spin, both off- and leg-breaks, and he could bowl a googly. *Wisden* remarked of his 1934 season that 'the absence of Staples afforded more opportunities to Gunn who showed such skill in spinning the ball, mainly from leg, that [he was used] as a stock bowler . . . Gunn and Voce expended so much energy in bowling that some falling off with the bat was almost inevitable.'

As it happens, 1934 was G.V.'s best season with the ball. He had taken 47 wickets in 1933 and the 77 of the following season suggested that he was about to become a major force among Notts bowlers. But as his batting advanced his bowling fell away and from 1935 until 1939 he made over 1,000 runs a season, and he became a valuable middle-order

Ben Lilley, Harold Larwood and George Vernon at the nets at Trent Bridge in April 1935.

batsman. One innings of 1935 is especially worthy of note. It was against Essex and G.V. made 147 not out which, *Wisden* reports, 'was the highest score of his career [to date] . . . He claimed 147 of 275 in three hours, forty minutes. He played the fast bowling particularly well and often walked down the pitch to Read.' No need to wonder where that tactic came from.

Young George's best season with the bat was 1937. In that summer he scored 1,763 runs at an average of 44.08 and according to *Wisden* 'seldom failed . . . he could adapt himself to the needs of the moment, particularly when runs were wanted quickly. He was very consistent that year.' He did not do so well in 1938, although his 184 against Leicester-shire was not only his highest score in first-class cricket, it was also the highest score made by any Notts batsman that summer. The following year he had scored 1,156 runs (average 31.24) and taken 31 wickets (at 40.25 each) when war was declared.

That year the *Nottingham Guardian* carried a series entitled 'The Gunns of Notts and England'. Of young George, the newspaper said:

> Great things were naturally expected from a son of George and a relative of the other great Gunns. He was coached by his father and has of course learned much from him; one thing is certain, no coaching has cramped his style. He remains the farmer's boy of Notts cricket.
>
> He goes in without artifice or after thought and lifts Copson into the pavilion quite naturally. All the critics have accused him of over-confidence; it is his greatest asset ... Who is this Gregory – or this Copson anyway? If I hit the ball hard enough, it will go for four. So he is seen at his best picking up twenties or thirties in a crisis.
>
> Of his bowling we have said a little; he commands both spins and is completely undisturbed by punishment. He fields admirably.

It is easy enough to detect the vein of disappointment that runs underneath those words of apparent praise; but it is necessary to speak up in G.V.'s defence. Being George's son, great things were inevitably expected of him. And if he pretended to see in that a challenge he must also have known it to be a burden. For how could he live up to such expectations? His father was inimitable. It says much for G.V.'s resilience of spirit that he was able to carry on playing an important part in the Notts side in spite of the numbers of wiseacres who would have been telling him that he wasn't half the man his father had been. Where some have seen an improper confidence in his own abilities it is probably better to admire an unwavering determination to continue in the face of what must have been continuing disappointments and the realisation, which he must have carried deep down within him, that he was never going to be the equal of those great Gunns who had gone before him.

In 1932, the year that George and John's first-class careers ended, John's wife died. Grace Gunn had been ill for some time with Bright's disease, and that year it finally killed her. The following year John remarried. We know very little about his second wife, apart from the fact that she was called Lucy and seems to have been of independent means. 'Wealthy' some have said, but this is probably an overstatement. Mrs Ann Coulthard, who as a girl knew Grace Gunn very well, and who often called in on the Gunn household between 1917 and 1930, says that Lucy was a cricket enthusiast and that she followed the Notts team on their away matches. Both she and Eric Gunn have told us that after the marriage John went to live at Lucy's house, 62 Edward Road, West Bridgford. He would live there for the rest of his life.

From Edward Road it was the shortest of walks to Trent Bridge, where John still spent much of his time. He was employed at the indoor nets, together with his friends Jim Iremonger and Sam Staples, and although increasingly corpulent and in a general way slow moving, his eye was still remarkably keen, as were his reflexes. Ken Wheatley recalls an incident which illustrates this fact. Aapparently a promising young fast bowler was one day bowling in the nets to the even younger Wheatley. Try as he might, he could not get the batsman out. The faster he bowled the more obdurate and determined Ken Wheatley became. John looked on, laughing. At last, infuriated beyond reason, the bowler turned round and hurled the ball at John, who was standing a few feet away. In an instant John's hand was up and he caught the ball. 'You'd didn't think I could do that, did you?' he asked the discomforted bowler.

In these years John was still employed by Sir Julien Cahn and regularly umpired for Cahn's XI. And as often as possible he watched his beloved Notts, although their performances cannot have given him unalloyed

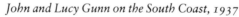

John and Lucy Gunn on the South Coast, 1937

pleasure. For in the later 1930s Notts did not have the success that should have come to a team so rich in ability. The decline starts with the dismissal of Carr in 1934, after the row about Bodyline tactics, in which the Notts committee upheld complaints by Lancashire and the Australians that Voce, in particular, had used unfair tactics against them. Carr backed his fast bowler. The upshot of the row was that Carr was removed from the captaincy and ceased to play. With his going much of the spirit went from Notts. They still played good cricket, but they were no longer a power in the land.

As for George, after his retirement he became for a while landlord of a Bass House pub, The Bentinck Hotel, which stands on a corner of Carrington Street across from the Midland Station and obliquely across from the original site of Gunn & Moore. The Bentinck was of course connected with cricket not just because of the man it was named after but because it was there that William Gunn had met his second wife. Now that George had become landlord numerous people associated with cricket would call in for a drink and a chat. Jimmy Haynes recalls meeting George Headley there. He autographed a bat for Jimmy's infant son, who, during the 1950s, played for Notts. The famous and the not-so-famous made it a regular port of call.

As we might expect, George was at once the most charming and the most feckless of landlords. 'I did the worrying so that he could go to the wicket,' Flo would tell Frank Stokes years later; but she must have had her share of worries over the running of the Bentinck. In the first place, George rarely remembered to call 'Time'. 'He wouldn't be flouting the law,' Joe Hardstaff told us. 'But he'd get yarning and four o'clock 'd come along and the doors 'd still be wide open.'

'Didn't the police complain?'

'No,' Joe said. 'They just took it for granted. It was old George. A copper 'd poke his head round the door and say "way over time, Mr Gunn," and that was it.'

Some of his yarning became expensive. Indeed, just before he died his younger son told us that George had said that one customer cost him three hundred Guinnesses. Claude Westall was at that time a Nottingham journalist – he later moved to the *Birmingham Post*. He wrote under the name of 'Claudius' and he had the idea of helping George to compose his autobiography. Either that, or he simply fancied talking and drinking with the great man. At all events, over a period of months Westall would make daily visits to the Bentinck and would consume Guinness after Guinness while listening to George's life story. Whether anything was ever committed to paper we do not know. It was certainly never published. If there was an 'as-told-to' life it disappeared with Westall.

George suffered another loss at this time. Bolton Wanderers were due at the City Ground to play Nottingham Forest in a cup tie and the police warned George to take care of his pewter tankards on that occasion. Naturally George forgot, with the result that the morning after the match he had no pewter tankards left.

Yet he cannot have done too badly. A grand piano was installed in the upstairs rooms and there were regular sing-songs and recitals. And he was now a car owner. Pauline Manders recalls George giving her rides in his green Packard and that often if she called in at the pub on her way back from school her grandfather would drive her down to the creamery so they could buy cream for tea.

Then there was George Gunn United. George had formed in 1929 an occasional cricket team and after his retirement it became his pride and joy. Billy Flint and Albert Iremonger played for it, as did Jimmy Haynes and several other good club cricketers. John and Eric Gunn also made occasional appearances. Another regular had no great abilities but was necessary for a different reason. Harry Buill, a master baker, loved his cricket, although Jimmy can remember him only once holding a catch and he did not bat or bowl. However, he owned a large Buick and since the team played all its matches away and he could take at least six of them in his car, George Gunn United rarely took the field without him.

For the most part the matches were against club or invitation elevens and were keenly contested. Jimmy Haynes can remember one occasion, however, in which George was less than keen to win. The match was against Squire Finch's XI (the Squire Finch who last rode to hounds at the age of 94). It was an all-day affair and by the middle of the afternoon George's team were doing well. Far too well. As Jimmy recalls it, George came into their changing-room a worried man. 'Lads,' he said. 'We've got to lose this match somehow.'

'Why?' they asked.

'Well,' George said, 'If we lose we shall be invited up to the hall afterwards and we'll have a cold collation fit for Buckingham Palace. And if we win,' and here he paused impressively, 'if we win we'll get the same sodding sandwiches as we had this morning.' Apparently Albert Iremonger hated to lose at anything, but on this one occasion even he saw

George and Flo with Pauline at Yarmouth, 1938.

◆ ● ➤

sense. The meal that followed was everything George had promised it would be.

George and Flo stayed at the Bentinck until 1939. But with war fast approaching the pub began to look increasingly vulnerable. Quite apart from the fact that it was next door to the railway station it was also close to the main Boots factory. It was therefore a prime target for German bombers.

On one occasion, indeed, both George and Flo assumed the war had begun. On 8 July 1939 the *Nottingham Journal* carried a headline *Nottingham Inquiry Office Roof Blown Away*, and the report underneath explained that an explosion had taken place at about 6.30 a.m. which had 'caused considerable damage to luggage and station property, but no injury to anyone'. The bomb had in fact been planted by the IRA, but George and Flo were not to know that. They were woken by the blast and according to the *Journal* reporter George's first impression was

15 Mapperley Hall Drive, George and Flo's last home.

◆●◆

'They've started. I thought it was from "upstairs" they'd dropped one,' he added. The reporter continues:

> His wife had experienced the same thing in 1915 while living in London, and she knew from the concussion that it was a bomb. 'It's a kind of expanding sensation with a bomb,' she added. 'I would know one anywhere. When I found out what it was, I was rather cross about it!

Very soon afterwards George retired from the pub and bought a house, 15 Mapperley Hall Drive, very near to the cemetery where his uncle lay buried. It was to be his and Flo's last home.

186

12

ENDINGS

With the outbreak of war, G.V. volunteered for active service. To his consternation and bitter disappointment he was turned down. The reason, his daughter believes, was 'water on the knee . . . which caused him . . . quite a bit of trouble.' He was however soon involved with war work, and he moved his family from West Bridgford to Grantham, where he managed a gun-barrel factory.

County cricket had, of course, been suspended, but a good deal of representative cricket was still being played, and would continue to be so throughout the war years. In August 1941 G.V. played for an Army XI against Sir Julien Cahn's XI in the last match ever played by that celebrated team. He did little to distinguish himself on that occasion, although G. F. H. Heane did hit him over the pavilion for a massive six.

In 1943 G.V. began to play for Keighley, in the Bradford League. The following summer the family moved yet again, this time to the Queens Hotel, Bridge Street, Bradford, G.V. having become manager of the hotel. No doubt a member of the Keighley committee had arranged for the post to be offered to him. Presumably he doubled cricket with the day-to-day affairs of running his hotel, and proof of how the two coincided comes with a photograph which shows him in the company of some Keighley members. On the back is scribbled a hotel menu. It reads: *sardines on toast, jam tart, rhubarb tart, chicken.*

When he went into Bradford League cricket G.V. was doing much as his father had done in the previous war. And so were many others. For among those cricketers who at some time or another during the Second World War played in the league were: Eddie Paynter (who also played for Keighley), Len Hutton, Les Ames, Jim Smith, George Pope and Bill Copson. And there were others. As a result standards were high and the competition fierce. In 1944 G.V.'s batting average for Keighley was 32, which put him no higher than sixteenth in the league averages, and Keighley finished bottom of Division A.

John Gunn no doubt followed his nephew's fortunes. He had little else to do. For the ending of Cahn's XI marked his final rupture with the playing of the game. He and Lucy continued to live at Edward Road, and he did his best to keep himself informed of such cricket as there was. For the rest there were evenings of reminiscence with old cricketing friends and the chance to pore over his collection of *Wisden*.

George, however, was far more active. From a letter written to the *Nottingham Evening Post* just after his death, we know that during the war years he was employed on the inspection staff of George Brough's factory at Vernon Road, Basford – the very road where Flo's father had worked. According to the correspondent, Ron W. Storey, George must have laid up his Packard, for he,

> cycled from his house each day, worked a shift from 9 a.m. to 4 p.m. and his pleasant disposition endeared him to all that he came into contact with. Many of the men and women who passed through George Brough's works during the early 1940s will recall the pleasure that

◄ ● ►

George Vernon at the ground at Keighley.

meeting and working along with George gave to them. His stock of stories about cricket, Test matches and his world travels, helped to brighten many of the dull, dreary days and the 12 hour shifts of the early years of the last war. He was truly a great all-rounder.

It was not only his workmates who valued his conversation. Albert Underwood, a Nottingham umpire who stood in many representative matches during the war years, remembers that whenever a guest team was due at Trent Bridge a call would go out to the Notts secretary, H. A. Brown, asking for George to umpire. 'They all wanted to talk to him,' Underwood recalled. 'Well, he didn't much like umpiring, but he'd often do it till teatime – usually wearing a pair of wellies which I had to pull on and off for him – and then he'd pack up and go. But they all loved to hear the tales he'd tell about his cricketing days.'

On one occasion, at least, George lasted beyond the tea interval. In 1943 a Notts XI played a two-day match against the All-England Fire Services XI. The Services XI included Warwickshire's C. Adderley, a defensive batsman who apparently gave an exemplary display of his particular skills until he was struck on his front pad by John Hodgkins. More in hope than belief Hodgkins appealed and, to his delight and the batsman's evident disgust, George raised his finger. During the pause before the next batsman arrived at the crease George sauntered over to the other umpire. 'Looked a bit close from square leg,' Albert Underwood suggested, tactfully. 'Oh, he wasn't out,' George said, 'not by a long chalk. But I was sick and tired of the way he was poking about.'

George also managed to play a few games for George Gunn United, and in 1941 only bad weather prevented him from putting his own XI into the field at Trent Bridge, their planned opponents being an Army XI. George's extremely strong XI included himself, Ben Lilley, Cyril Lowater, Reg Simpson, Frank Shipstone and J. Corch. Sadly, continuous rain prevented so much as a ball being bowled.

In 1943 George watched a game of baseball. There were thousands of American troops in Nottingham by that time and one afternoon two teams of US servicemen arranged a match on Notts County's ground at Meadow Lane. Eric Penson, who was there at the time, recalls sitting near George among the small crowd. The game began at half-past two and by six o'clock neither side had managed a home run, so, Mr Penson writes, 'George got up, stretched his legs and said, "They can have this game, for me," and we all went home.'

189

It might be supposed that with the end of the war G.V. would return to the Notts staff. But he decided not to do so. Instead, he announced that he would continue to play for Keighley. He was by now 40 years old, and he probably felt that his future in the game lay outside county cricket. League cricket paid well, he could continue to run his hotel and there might always be opportunities for coaching, at home or abroad. In 1947 he moved to Pudsey, as captain, but after a poor season he was not retained. That summer he played two matches in the Hastings Festival: for South v North, when he opened for South and scored 32 and 30; and for Maurice Leyland's XI v The Rest, when he made 15 and 35. He was to play one other first-class match. In 1950 Notts suffered a number of

George Vernon and Pauline, January 1945.

injuries and in some desperation they asked both Bill Voce and G.V. to play for them in the match against Derbyshire at Trent Bridge. It was a dismal failure as far as G.V. was concerned. In his one innings he was bowled by Rhodes for nought. It was a decent career but, like so much in his life, it came to a sad end.

His marriage, for example. According to his daughter, Pauline, his wife left him in 1949 for another man:

> for a long time he was inconsolable. At this time my older brother David was already on his own, I went to live with my grandparents, and my younger brother Michael stayed in boarding school, spending some holidays with my grandparents, and eventually going to live with my mother. Dad took various jobs coaching cricket [which included going to] British West Guiana to coach the government officials there for a season. After he came back he had several 'lady friends', and finally met Joyce, whom he eventually married. She was quite a bit younger than him, but they were very happy together.

In 1950 he became coach at Wrekin College. He seems to have been happy there. Between 1953 and 1955 he acted as coach to Worcestershire. He and Joyce lived latterly in a caravan at Leegomery, Shropshire, and when they travelled it was on his motorbike. We have already seen

◄ ● ►

George Vernon with some pupils at Wrekin College.

that he was accident-prone; and in October 1957 he died, having received serious head injuries when he was thrown from his motorbike. Joyce, who was riding pillion, escaped with minor cuts and bruises.

After his son's death, George wrote to John Arlott, clearly in reply to a letter of condolence, and in the course of the letter he said that G.V. 'had three smashes really, and they say third time pays for all.' It is a stoical, even resigned letter, perhaps because this was the second death of a close relative that George had had to endure within a year. There may even be a tinge of disappointed expectations masquerading as hardness in the letter. G.V. was never the cricketer that his father had wanted him to be; he was never the cricketer that he himself had wanted to be. Of course, he was a good average county cricketer. But to be a Gunn and to be no more was to be a failure – in his own eyes and perhaps, just perhaps, in his father's, too. It may well be that the difficulties of being George's son outweighed the advantages. Neither is to be blamed for this, but it makes it easier to understand why George's other son, in spite of some early promise, never seriously thought of trying to make a career out of cricket. It says much for young George's character that, in spite of his failure to achieve the distinction that he and perhaps his father desired for him, he remained the most cheerful of cricketers and companions.

In 1953 John's second wife, Lucy, died. If, as we have suggested, she had been a woman of some means when she married John, by the time she died they had either exhausted her money or she left it elsewhere. For after her death he fashioned for himself a bachelor existence of very modest means. He continued to live at Edward Road, and he went to Trent Bridge as often as possible – frequently growling his disapproval of the players of the day. A correspondent remembers him remarking, as one Notts unfortunate returned to the pavilion after a dismal innings: 'that fellow's the best allrounder I've ever seen. He can't bat, he can't bowl, and he can't bloody-well field.' He also began a correspondence with a young admirer from New Zealand, Robin McConnell, who had written to him to ask for a photograph and for anything John might care to tell him about his career or his thoughts on cricket and cricketers, past and present. As so often with old men, John preferred the past. 'Every county team is going down a bit in England,' he wrote in one letter of 1958. 'Fancy, we cannot find a couple to go in first for England, at one time . . . we could have picked three teams and you would not know which one was the best . . .'

In spite of the grumbles his love of the game did not diminish. He continued to study *Wisden*, and Peter Townsend can remember going round to Edward Road on a Sunday and seeing his grandfather, plate of beef, roast potatoes ('tatties' he always called them) and peas in front of him, a *Wisden* at one elbow, bottle of beer at the other, reading with such intense concentration that his food was cold before he remembered its existence. He also remembers the occasion when his grandfather wrote him a congratulatory postcard, after he had scored 79 for his club, Forest Wanderers, against Chilwell Garrison. 'Dear Peter,' John wrote, 'was very pleased to see you had made your first (50) in fact 79 very good indeed . . . You must play your own game and take no notice of anyone telling you what to do.'

'When I die it'll all be forgotten,' he once said to Peter; and he was rightly irritated when people failed to remember his great achievements. On 17 August 1956 he wrote to John Arlott:

> Dear John,
>
> Some time ago Mr J. Swanton gave out on the wireless about our left arm bowler A. K. Walker, when he did the (hat-trick) in the first three balls of the second innings. He said it was a world record, never been done before. I did it some years ago at Chesterfield against Derby claiming the wickets of L. G. Wright, C. Ollivierre and W. Storer in the first three balls of the second innings same as Walker.
>
> Thought you might have a word or two with Mr Swanton and put him right . . .

'Some years ago' was in fact 1904, and it appears John's memory isn't quite accurate. He certainly took the wickets he claims and they provided him with a hat-trick. But he must have bowled the second over of the innings, because there were already some runs on the board when he dismissed the three Derbyshire batsmen. In view of the fact that he was 80 when he wrote the letter the slip is understandable.

George, of course, was by no means a forgotten man. Indeed, he was rapidly becoming a legend. He was also performing valuable work for his county. In 1945 Notts, like so many counties, were in very poor financial circumstances. They decided to campaign for 4,500 new members and George was co-opted onto the committee set up to run the campaign. He was also made a member of the full Notts committee and took his duties very seriously. He served on the club and ground and selection sub-committees and from minute books it is clear that he was a regular 193 attender at meetings. He also had a remit to keep an eye on promising young players around the county. And of course his neat, dapper figure, invariably dressed in brown suit and trilby could be seen at all the county matches. Grahame Booker recalls him, immaculate in his suit and rolled umbrella, sauntering into the pavilion and enquiring as to the state of play. 'In the decade after the war when the fortunes of Notts were at a pretty low ebb, the answer was frequently decidedly gloomy. "Never mind," said George, settling into his seat, "the fresh air will do 'em good."'

He was accorded some honours. *Wisden* records that on 14 July 1949,

> The Duke of Edinburgh was in the chair at a Special General Meeting [of MCC] ... when it was decided unanimously to offer Honorary Cricket Membership to a select number of English Professionals who had retired from the game. The Duke emphasised that the election would be restricted to the really great and would be a genuine recognition of their services to the game and to the MCC in particular.

Offers were eventually made to 26 old players, one of them being George Gunn. Not to be outdone, in 1955 his own county made him honorary life vice-president of the club.

While he no doubt enjoyed his modest fame – he gave fairly regular interviews in the press and on the radio – the intense happiness of his family life was at the heart of all he did. Pauline Manders, who lived with her grandparents from the age of 16 to 22, when she married and went to Canada, has provided us with a close, deeply affectionate view of George and Flo in retirement.

> To really know Poppa, you have to remember the old adage about 'behind every great man, there is a woman' and in their case it was very true. I doubt anyone ever knew how much he cared for and relied on her. He was very much a 'man's man' but very shy with the ladies. She was the business manager in the family, and thanks to her they lived a very comfortable retirement for nearly 25 years.

> She loved to play bridge and on the afternoons she was going to be late she'd tell me what was for tea and say for us to go ahead and eat without her. But there was no way I could convince him to eat until she came home. He was like a lost soul without her.

Four generations of Gunns – George and Flo with George Vernon, Pauline and Pauline's daughter, Debi Sue, 1955.

Pauline adds that George, surprisingly, was colour-blind and that Flo had a hard time of it getting him to match his ties and shirts. And she also remembers that Flo 'was always rushing around and doing things full speed ahead. His favourite reply when she was trying to hurry him up to go somewhere was, "take your time, you'll get there just the same," and they always did.'

As to his eating habits, Pauline recalls that,

> The first thing he did to the food on his plate was practically bury it in salt and pepper, and to this day I can still hear Granny lecturing him and threatening to feed him 'burnt toast' as she was sure he couldn't taste anything . . . after which lecture he would wink at me and give the pepper shaker one more shake – just to get a rise out of her.

> He was a beautiful pianist, and one of my fondest memories is walking home along Mapperley Hall Drive after work, in the summer when the windows were open, and hearing him play his favourite music . . . he had a beautiful touch, he loved to play, you could tell just by the way he touched the keys.

Frank Stokes, George's close neighbour during those years, also remembers George with great affection. 'Oh, he was a hero of mine. I'd seen him when I was a boy playing his wonderful innings, so to have him living at the back of my house was a great thrill.' George was a great raconteur. 'He'd come to the fence and tell me extraordinary tales of his great days.' George coached his two small sons. 'He'd make them play very straight, head down, nose over the ball. "Don't look up to Jesus" he'd say, if they lifted their heads.' And he would take them down to the nearby police ground, where he acted as unpaid coach to the powerful Notts Police XI.

As the 1950s wore on Flo weakened. 'She was often under the weather,' Mr Stokes recalls, and we know from Pauline Manders that she suffered increasingly from arthritis of the knees. She wrote to Pauline for Christmas 1956, telling her that she and George were going to their son, John's, for the festive season. 'Much love to you all and hope to see you again, when your ship comes in,' she ended her letter. Shortly after, she fell heavily, was rushed to hospital, and there she died, on 19 December.

George was shattered. Pauline and her husband wrote to invite him over to Canada and in reply he thanked them but said:

> I feel as though the bottom has dropped out of everything, lost the toss and batting one short all the time. Anyway there is nothing we can do about it. Granny stuck it very well the last three years, in pain all the time, and it was a blessing in a way when she passed on. She used to say Don't grieve for me now, don't grieve for me ever, I'm going to do nothing for ever and ever. But that takes a bit of doing. But she was such a merry soul when she was fit and I must say, she had a good innings . . .

Then came G.V.'s death and with it George lost much of his zest for living. He still went to Trent Bridge and he even planned to visit Australia with the touring MCC side of 1958–59. He wrote to a niece, Molly Meek (her mother was Flo's sister), who was in Australia, suggesting he might stay with her and she wrote back excitedly, telling him how much she was looking forward to seeing him. But he now looked a very old man indeed.

On 24 June 1958 he and his brother parted outside the main gates at Trent Bridge, after the end of the game against Yorkshire. 'See you at the next match,' George said to John. Before then he was due to spend a few days at Cuckfield, Sussex, the home of his son, John. On 28 June he complained to his son of chest pains, went to bed, and died in his sleep.

John Stapleton Gunn arranged for his father's funeral to take place in Sussex, but when John senior got to hear of it he would not allow it.

George and John together at Trent Bridge in the late 1950s.

'They'll have to scatter his ashes at Trent Bridge, or he'll never rest,' Flo had once told Frank Stokes, and John Gunn now said to Peter Townsend, 'George will be buried where he lived – in Nottingham.' The body was brought home and George's remains were cremated at Wilford Hills. His funeral drew a large crowd and his death was marked by numerous obituaries. Perhaps the most touching was the funeral oration delivered by H. A. Brown in which, having paid tribute to 'George Gunn, the incomparable,' he concluded: 'We shall not see his like again, but his name and fame will live on in cricket history as a great player and in our hearts as a gentle-man. May he rest in peace.'

So now John was left alone, the last of the Gunns. In 1960 he wrote to Pauline and her husband, 'It seems very funny now for me to go to cricket without George, they are all gone now, the Gunns.' That year he had his portrait painted by his grandson, John Townsend, Peter's brother and a portrait painter of some standing. The picture was presented to Trent Bridge, where it now hangs in the long-room. It shows John in dignified old age, the eyes humorous, the mouth and chin determined.

The following year he was invited to Lord's for a special Lord's Taverners lunch and, after some hesitation, accepted. He had an enjoyable time, but somehow lost his false teeth on the journey home.

Even he, although physically the toughest of the family, was becoming frail. He walked with the help of a stick and he complained of the cold. During the long, hard winter of 1962–63 Notts helped him out by giving him an allowance with which to buy his coal. But the end was near. One day Peter Townsend called in to see his grandfather and found him sitting immobile in his chair. The old man was uncommunicative and seemed to be in some pain. Moreover, Peter detected an odd smell in the air. Alarmed, he summoned Eric, John's son. Eric suggested that they send for a doctor. When he came he made a quick examination and told them that John had gangrene in his right leg.

John was taken to hospital and the surgeons agreed to amputate his leg below the knee. The news was, however, kept from John himself. Eric recalls arriving at the hospital to find his father being wheeled away from the operating theatre, without the operation having been performed. 'He wouldn't allow it when he realised what they intended,' Eric said, adding, 'If you've been a great sportsman you don't want to lose a limb.' It appears that the old man was ready to die, and that he wished to die in some dignity. Peter and Eric accompanied him back to his bed. As he lay there he began muttering about Billy Flint's boots. 'His mind was in the past,' Eric said, 'He must have borrowed Bill Flint's boots at some time, and he wanted to make sure we would return them!'

Then something strange and immeasurably moving happened. As John lay on his deathbed he raised his left arm slightly and began to flex his wrist. 'We couldn't think what he was up to,' Peter said, 'We could see his fingers moving as though they were holding, feeling something. And then it dawned on us. He'd got a ball in his hand. He was making to bowl.'

On 21 August 1963 the last of the cricketing Gunns died.

THE GUNNS IN FIRST-CLASS CRICKET

Compiled by Simon Wilde

WILLIAM GUNN

1880 to 1904

	Innings	Not Outs	Runs	Highest Score	100s	Average
1880	22	5	183	29*	—	10.76
1881	32	3	554	91	—	19.10
1882	25	4	426	188	1	20.29
1883	34	1	740	77	—	22.42
1884	27	2	647	138	2	25.88
1885	43	3	1,451	203	1	36.28
1886	31	3	752	83	—	26.86
1886–87 (Australia)	17	1	473	150	1	29.56
1887	30	3	958	205*	1	35.48
1888	47	2	920	91	—	20.44
1889	40	5	1,319	118	1	37.69
1890	53	6	1,621	228	3	34.49
1891	37	5	1,336	169	4	41.75
1892	39	2	1,120	103	1	30.27
1893	51	3	2,057	156	7	42.85
1894	38	1	1,112	121*	2	30.05
1895	31	0	920	219	2	29.68
1896	38	7	1,383	207*	3	44.61
1897	32	3	1,266	230	4	43.66
1898	36	5	1,484	236*	4	47.87
1899	39	2	1,392	150	2	37.62
1900	28	3	887	137	2	35.48
1901	20	1	751	273	2	39.53
1902	24	1	807	120	3	35.09
1903	29	1	1,011	139	2	36.11
1904	7	0	121	39	—	17.29
TOTALS	850	72	25,691	273	48	33.02

William Gunn also took in first-class cricket 76 wickets at 23.68 runs each and 333 catches and 1 stumping.

Highest score: 273 Notts v Derbyshire, Derby, 1901

Best bowling: 6 for 48 Notts v Hampshire, Southampton, 1885

TEST CRICKET

	M	Inns	NO	Runs	HS	100s	Average
1886–87 to 1899	11	20	2	392	102*	1	21.78

Did not bowl and 5 catches

Highest score: 102 not out England v Australia, Old Trafford, 1893

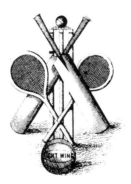

JOHN GUNN

1896 to 1932

	Inns	NO	Runs	HS	100s	Av	Runs	Wkts	Av
1896	2	1	12	12*	—	12.00	—	—	—
1897	13	4	209	107	1	23.22	460	15	30.67
1898	17	5	183	47	—	15.25	769	25	30.76
1899	24	5	327	60	—	17.21	1,290	56	23.04
1900	38	8	734	70	—	24.47	2,523	115	21.94
1901	39	3	1,317	91	—	36.58	2,154	92	23.41
1901–02 (Australia)	16	2	154	30	—	11.04	769	29	26.52
1902	32	3	652	80	—	22.48	1,672	73	22.90
1903	42	3	1,665	294	3	42.69	2,283	118	19.35
1904	43	3	1,225	100	1	30.63	3,109	123	25.28
1905	43	5	1,366	178	3	35.95	2,827	111	25.47
1906	41	2	1,395	112	2	35.77	2,427	112	21.67
1907	34	6	913	109	3	32.61	1,126	38	29.63
1908	27	2	688	144*	1	27.52	674	22	30.64
1909	36	4	874	110*	1	27.31	677	22	30.77
1910	33	5	861	93*	—	30.75	298	14	21.29
1911	35	3	1,368	160	3	42.75	1,683	49	34.35
1912	31	3	975	113	3	34.82	387	13	29.77
1913	38	6	1,405	126	3	43.91	844	31	27.23
1914	34	5	1,358	154*	3	46.83	992	37	26.81
1919	24	5	903	111*	2	47.53	396	20	19.80
1920	35	5	1,299	131	4	43.30	306	12	25.50
1921	40	5	1,178	148	2	33.66	1,317	51	25.82
1922	38	3	923	150	2	26.37	707	38	18.61
1923	34	3	1,173	116*	1	37.84	152	7	21.71
1924	39	6	969	113	1	29.36	457	18	25.39
1925	13	0	332	166	1	25.54	30	0	—
1929–30 (S America)	2	0	97	70	—	48.50	87	2	43.50
1932	2	0	2	2	—	1.00	47	1	47.00
TOTALS	845	105	24,557	294	40	33.19	30,463	1,242	24.53

John Gunn also took 248 catches in first-class cricket.
Highest score: 294 Notts v Leics, Trent Bridge, 1903
Best bowling: 8 for 63 Notts v Surrey, Oval, 1903

TEST CRICKET

	M	Inns	NO	Runs	HS	100s	Average	Runs	Wkts	Average
1901–02 to 1905	6	10	2	85	24	–	10.62	387	18	21.50

3 catches
Highest score: 24 England v Australia, Adelaide, 1901–02
Best bowling: 5 for 76 England v Australia, Adelaide, 1901–02

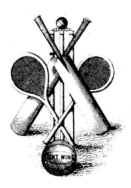

GEORGE GUNN

1902 to 1932

	Innings	Not Outs	Runs	Highest Score	100s	Average
1902	7	4	65	20*	—	21.67
1903	34	6	660	59	—	23.57
1904	31	4	797	143	2	29.52
1905	43	4	1,278	126	2	32.77
1906	26	1	775	113	1	31.00
1907	32	3	949	84	—	32.72
1907–08 (Australia)	18	3	817	122*	4	54.47
1908	50	4	1,432	129	2	31.13
1909	40	2	1,170	138	2	30.79
1910	38	2	1,013	98	—	28.14
1911	42	1	1,577	143	1	38.46
1911–12 (Australia)	15	2	665	106	1	51.15
1912	32	1	743	76	—	23.97
1913	39	5	1,697	170	6	49.91
1914	42	2	1,297	104*	2	32.43
1919	25	2	1,451	185*	5	63.09
1920	30	0	1,050	112	2	35.00
1921	44	3	1,647	138	3	40.17
1922	48	3	1,464	180*	2	32.53
1923	42	2	1,439	220	3	35.98
1924	48	3	1,414	112	1	31.42
1925	45	4	1,573	117	2	38.37
1926	34	3	1,192	191	2	38.45
1927	48	3	1,790	116	3	39.78
1928	52	4	1,933	159	6	40.27
1929	50	2	1,788	178	4	37.25
1929–30 (West Indies)	17	0	707	178	1	41.59
1930	43	4	1,276	129	2	32.72
1931	39	5	1,329	183	3	39.09
1932	7	0	220	74	—	31.43
TOTALS	1061	82	35,208	220	62	35.96

George Gunn also took in first-class cricket 66 wickets at 35.68 runs each and 473 catches.
Highest score: 220 Notts v Derbyshire, Trent Bridge, 1923
Best bowling: 5 for 50 Notts v Middlesex, Trent Bridge, 1905

TEST CRICKET

	M	Inns	NO	Runs	HS	100s	Average
1907–08 to 1929–30	15	29	1	1,120	122*	2	40.00

0 wickets for 8 runs and 15 catches
Highest score: 122 not out England v Australia, Sydney, 1907–08

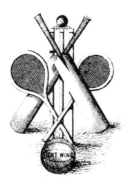

G. V. GUNN

1928 to 1950

	Innings	Not Outs	Runs	Highest Score	100s	Average
1928	3	0	24	10	—	8.00
1929	11	1	199	73	—	19.90
1930	11	0	221	66	—	20.09
1931	26	5	620	100*	1	29.52
1932	36	5	774	89*	—	24.97
1933	35	6	793	62	—	27.34
1934	48	5	922	83	—	21.44
1935	39	4	1,286	147*	3	36.74
1936	45	3	1,107	93	—	26.36
1937	48	8	1,763	149*	3	44.08
1938	46	1	1,360	184	2	30.22
1939	42	5	1,156	119	2	31.24
1947	4	0	112	35	—	28.00
1950	1	0	0	0	—	0.00
TOTALS	395	43	10,337	184	11	29.37

G. V. Gunn also took in first-class cricket 281 wickets at 35.68 runs each and 115 catches.

Highest score: 184 Notts v Leics, Trent Bridge, 1938

Best bowling: 7 for 44 Notts v Essex, Trent Bridge, 1932

* signifies not out

Bibliography

H. S. Altham and E. W. Swanton. *A History of Cricket* (1947)

F. S. Ashley-Cooper. *Nottinghamshire Cricket and Cricketers* (Nottingham, 1923)

R. G. Barlow. *40 Years of First Class Cricket: Career and Reminiscences* (c.a. 1908)

Denzil Batchelor. *The Book of Cricket* (1952)

A. C. L. (Leo) Bennett. *The Weekend Cricketer* (1951)

Christopher Brookes. *English Cricket, The Game and its Players through the Ages* (Newton Abbot, 1978)

Badminton Library. *Cricket* (1940)

William Caffyn. *71 Not Out* (1899)

Neville Cardus. *A Cricketer's Book* (1929)

Neville Cardus. *Good Days* (1937)

A. W. Carr. *Cricket With the Lid Off* (1935)

Cricket: A Weekly Record of the Game

The Cricketer

Richard Daft. *Kings of Cricket* (Bolton, 1893)

Michael Down. *'Archie': A Biography of A. C. MacLaren* (1981)

Leslie Duckworth. *S. F. Barnes, Master Bowler* (1967)

W. J. Edrich. *Cricket Heritage* (1947)

David Frith. *'My Dear Victorious Stod': A Biography of A. E. Stoddart* (Guildford, 1977)

David Frith. *The Golden Age of Cricket* (Guildford, 1978)

David Foot. *Harold Gimblett, Tormented Genius of Cricket* (1982)

Roy Genders. *League Cricket in England* (1952)

W. G. Grace. *Cricketing Reminiscences and Personal Recollections* (1899)

John Gunn. *The Life of John Richmond Gunn* (unfinished memoirs c.a. 1934)

W. R. Hammond. *Cricket my Destiny* (1946)

W. R. Hammond. *Cricket my World* (1947)

W. R. Hammond. *Cricketers School* (1950)

W. R. Hammond. *Cricket's Secret History* (1952)

Lord Hawke. *Recollections and Reminiscences* (1924)

Jack Hobbs. *Playing For England, My Test Cricket Story* (1931)

Jack Hobbs. *My Life Story* (1935)

Gilbert Jessop. *A Cricketer's Log* (1923)

Lionel Kirk. *Personal Cuttings Books 1920–1929* (Trent Bridge, 1929)
Harold Larwood. *The Larwood Story* (Sportsmans Book Club, 1967)
E. V. Lucas. *A Hundred Years of Trent Bridge* (Nottingham, 1938)
James Lillywhite's Cricketer's Annual
John Lillywhite's Cricketers' Companion
Patrick Morrah. *Alfred Mynn and the Cricketers of His Time* (1963)
Nottinghamshire County Cricket Club Handbooks
Nottinghamshire County Cricket Club Minutes
Cecil Parkin. *Cricket Triumphs and Troubles* (Manchester, 1936)
Ian Peebles. *Batter's Castle, A ramble round the Realm of Cricket* (1958)
Ian Peebles. *Spinner's Yarn* (1977)
A. W. Pullin ('Old Ebor') *Shaw (A), His Career and Reminiscences* (1892)
K. S. Ranjitsinhji. *The Jubilee Book of Cricket* (1902)
C. H. Richards. *Nottinghamshire Cricket Scores and Biographies 1888–1900* (Nottingham, 1903)
Fred Root. *A Cricket Pro's Lot* (1937)
Gordon Ross. *Cricket's Great Characters* (1977)
Sydney Smith. *History of the Tests* (1946)
E. E. Snow. *Sir Julien Cahn's XI* (Leicester, 1964)
Herbert Strudwick. *25 Years Behind the Stumps* (1926)
Robert Trumble. *The Golden Age of Cricket: A Memorial Book of Hugh Trumble* (Melbourne, 1968)
P. F. Warner. *England v. Australia, 1912* (1912)
P. F. Warner. *My Cricketing Life* (c.a. 1932)
Sir Pelham Warner. *Cricket Between two Wars* (1942)
Sir Pelham Warner. *Lord's 1787–1945* (1946)
Roy Webber. *The Playfair Book of Test Cricket*. Vols 1 and 2 (1953)
Roy Webber. *The County Cricket Championship* (1957)
Wisden Cricketers' Almanack
Peter Wynne-Thomas. *Nottinghamshire Cricketers 1821–1914* (Nottingham, 1971)
Peter Wynne-Thomas. *Nottinghamshire Cricketers 1914–1939* (Nottingham, 1980)
Peter Wynne-Thomas. *England on Tour* (1982)